the KNITTER'S GUIDE to

HAND-DYED
AND
VARIEGATED
YARN

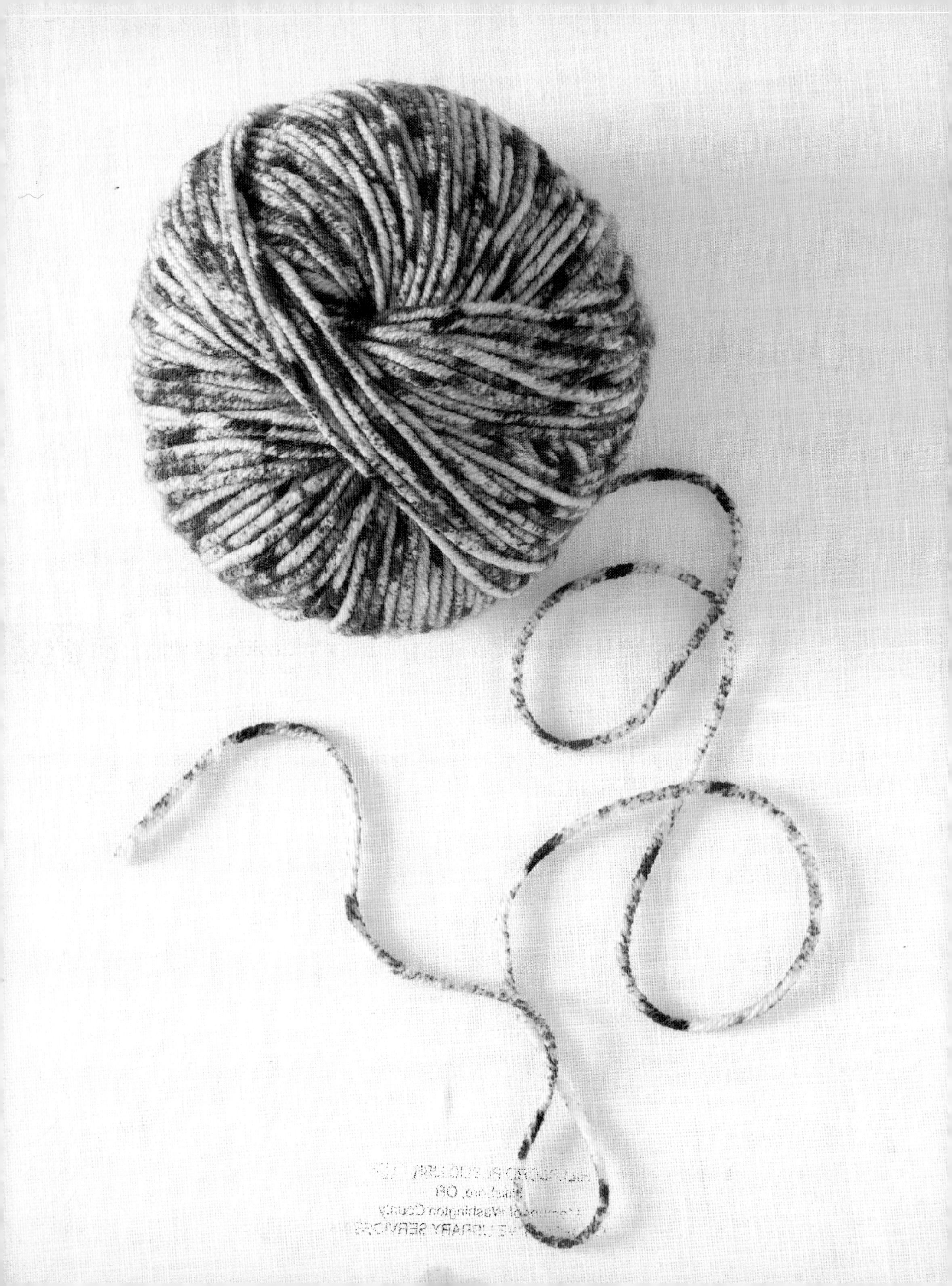

THE KNITTER'S GUIDE TO
HAND-DYED &
VARIEGATED YARN

Techniques and Projects for Hand-Painted and Multicolored Yarn

LORNA MISER

Founder of Lorna's Laces

Watson-Guptill Publications / New York

Published in the United States by Watson-Guptill Publications,
an imprint of the Crown Publishing Group,
a division of Random House, Inc., New York

www.crownpublishing.com
www.watsonguptill.com

Watson-Guptill is a registered trademark and WG and
Horse designs are trademarks of Random House, Inc.

Designed by veést design

ISBN 978-0-8230-8552-1

Printed in China

First Printing, 2010

1 2 3 4 5 6 7 8 9 / 18 17 16 15 14 13 12 11 10

Library of Congress Cataloging-in-Publication Data

Miser, Lorna.
  The knitter's guide to hand-dyed and variegated yarn : tech-
niques and projects for hand-painted and multicolored yarn /
Lorna Miser.
     p. cm.
  Includes bibliographical references and index.
  ISBN 978-0-8230-8552-1 (alk. paper) 45374195   3/11
1. Knitting--Patterns. 2. Dyes and dyeing--Textile fibers. I. Title.
TT825.M593 2010
  746.43'2041--dc22

                              2010002646

My hope is that this book will be a reference book for years to come.

So I am dedicating it to my three grandchildren,

Joe, Elly, and Deanna.

I love knitting for kids and, as their Nana, I should knit even more for them.
I love them and they inspire me and keep me young!

May this book still be useful and available when they are old enough to knit.

Acknowledgments

I would like to thank my talented knitters: Sheila Igoe, Mike Wren, Grace (Miser) Reidinger, Amy Harbach, Sally Gray, and Wes Thyberg. Also, thanks to Edie Eckman, Linda Hetzer, Autumn Kindelspire, and Joy Aquillino, who helped me throughout the project.

CONTENTS

Preface

I learned to knit in 1968 as a child, began knitting with a passion in 1982 when I became a mother, then started dyeing variegated yarns in 1986. Once I began knitting my hand-dyed yarns, I quickly discovered that they require extra thought and care to make them look as pretty when they're knitted into projects as they do in the skein. The colors that blend and flow so beautifully before they're knitted sometimes separate into patches or pools of color, or create stripes and zigzags. I never knew what "designs" a yarn might make, and even after knitting a swatch from one skein, there was no guarantee that the second skein would knit up the same way. Since I was selling those yarns, I needed to come up with tips and designs that would help knitters use them successfully. A happy knitter buys more yarn!

Many people enjoy the surprise of seeing the colors pool and swirl. If you like surprises, knit on! However, if you would prefer to have a bit of control over how the colors take shape, this book is here to help.

My goal for years has been to put together ten of the most common, simplest techniques that can significantly improve the way the colors in variegated yarns look after they're knitted. I learned that the same techniques work for all kinds of multicolored yarns, whether hand-dyed or commercially dyed. With this in mind, I devised *The Knitter's Guide to Hand-dyed and Variegated Yarn* as a stitch dictionary that specifically addresses the problems my students and I encountered when working with them.

Some of the techniques work to help jumble the colors together. Others mix the colors a little and make the pooling more subtle and attractive. Many techniques are useful, and there's certainly more than one approach to using these yarns. While other designers may use complex modular or intarsia techniques, my suggestions are very accessible, ranging from adding texture to mixing in solid colors. Of course, there are no right or wrong solutions, as long as you like the way your knitted project looks. I find, though, that it's nice to have some tools to choose from before casting on for a project. A little swatching and experimenting can be very eye-opening, and allow you to see some very different outcomes with the same yarn colors.

My hope is that this book will empower knitters to make informed decisions about how to show variegated yarns to their best advantage even before beginning a project, so they avoid disappointments and gain satisfaction with the beautiful color combinations and the exciting creative possibilities these yarns offer.

Lorna Miser

chapter

one

A LOOK AT MULTICOLORED YARNS

A Panorama of Color

Variegated yarn means multicolored yarn—essentially, many colors along a strand—a definition that encompasses many weights, fibers, and dyeing techniques. Sometimes a yarn will be labeled as hand-dyed or hand-painted. Regardless of whether a yarn is dyed by hand or commercially, there are similarities among the different types. These types reflect how long the color sections are and how soon the same color sequence occurs again, also referred to as the "repeat." This chapter gives an overview of the different styles of variegated yarns, whether hand-dyed or commercially dyed, and how they are made, for a better understanding of these yarns. Each of the following chapters offers different techniques and suggestions on how to use these yarns, which type of variegated colors will work with each technique, and two projects that show how the technique knits up.

Types of Variegated Yarn

Variegated yarn can be thought of as being one of three types: spotted or watercolor yarns; yarns with short repeats; and yarns with long repeats.

Spotted or Watercolor Yarns

These yarns have very tiny spots of color or the colors flow like water into each other. The colors change frequently, and there are often many colors in one skein. The repeats tend to be more random than defined, so the colors usually knit up in a pleasant, mixed, if busy, pattern. This type of dyeing is less likely to pool, but will still benefit from the techniques in this book. It is also important to consider how the colorway will work with a technique (see "Choosing the Right Knitting Technique for your Colorway" on page 20).

This yarn has been printed commercially to make very tiny color sections. It will knit into a spotted-looking fabric without pooling.

This is a commercially dyed wool. The color sections are short and gently flow into each other. Pooling would be subtle, if it happens at all.

This hand-dyed yarn is mainly blue with occasional spots of other colors. The colors are not likely to form pools.

The color sections in this hand-dyed yarn are short and have tiny spots of color mixed in. It will likely knit up without any substantial pooling.

Short-Repeat Yarns

The color sections in these yarns range from three to six inches long and usually repeat once or twice around a hank of yarn. This type of variegation is very common, and for hand-dyers, it's easy to create. The colors are poured from bottles onto sections of the skein or painted on with big brushes. Often the length of each color is about the same width as the dyer's hand because the colors are applied and then "kneaded" into the yarn by hand. Pooling is a good possibility with this type of dyeing and all the techniques in this book provide knitters with tools to take charge of the color outcome.

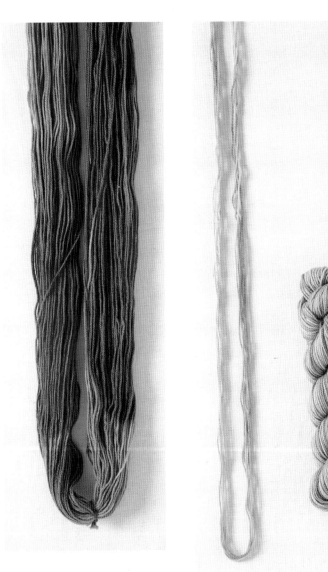

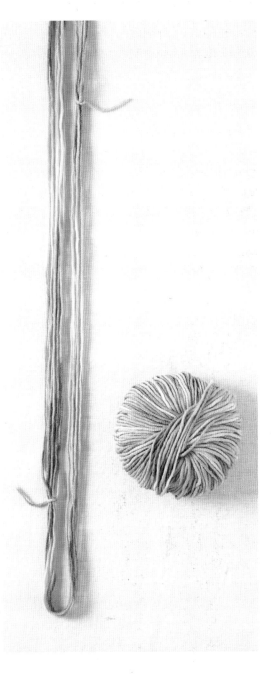

Even this commercially dyed colorway has a discernable repeat when it is unwound from the ball and the colors are lined up.

This hand-dyed yarn has only two colors, which makes it more likely for the colors to stack up when knit and for patterning or pooling to occur.

This hand-dyed yarn has been rewound into a different diameter loop than when it was dyed, which mixes the colors, making it very neat and attractive for purchase. By unwinding a few yards and rewinding them so that the colors line up, you can see how long the color sections are and how much of each color there is. It's apparent that there is very little green and a lot of pink, and it's likely the pink tones will pool when knit up.

Long-Repeat Yarns

Longer color repeats may be seven to twenty inches or more in length and, in a hank of yarn, the color might wrap halfway around the circle. More stitches can be knit with each color so they are very likely to pool. Hand-dyed yarns with long repeats are often dip-dyed, where part of the skein is dipped into a vat of dye in one color, and the remaining part is dipped in another color. Color sections this long are unusual in mass-produced yarns.

A similar-looking type of long-repeat yarn is dyed in a circle rather than flat. The colors repeat around the circle in one direction. Knitting from the other end of the ball will reverse the color order. This type of variegation is sometimes designed to pool intentionally. It can be knit in ways to blend the colors, though, using the techniques in this book.

Because this yarn is commercially dyed and packaged, it's deceptive in that it looks like the colors are short and will not pool. By unwinding a few yards and rewinding them so that the colors line up, you can see how similar it is to the yellow, green, and white sample (far right): There are two blue sections for each white and brown one. These colors will pool when knit.

This yarn has been hand-dyed, most likely by dipping each end into a separate color. This makes each color very long. The skein basically has only two colors, except for the slight blending where the colors meet. These colors will most definitely stack up and pool when knit, no matter what gauge or number of stitches is used.

This yarn has been dyed by hand, leaving part of the skein undyed. The yellow sections are shorter than the green and white, but there are two of them for each loop of the skein. These colors will almost definitely pool when knit.

Another commercially dyed yarn is wound into a center-pull skein that makes it appear as if the colors are distributed equally. By unwinding a few yards and rewinding them so that the colors line up, you can see that the color sections are quite long and the blue section is the longest. These colors will pool when knit.

In this brightly colored, hand-dyed rainbow yarn, each color overlaps the next one. The colors are only in one place on the skein, which means that the colors will knit up in one order from one end of the skein, and in the reverse color order when knit from the other end of the skein.

Striping or Self-Patterning Yarns

When each individual color is very long, from a couple of yards to many yards, the colors form stripes when knit. Originally, this type of yarn could be created only by dyeing the fiber before it was spun, then spinning each color individually for a length before adding the next color, a process that can be done by hand spinning or by commercial spinners. In recent years, however, methods for printing the colors onto yarn have been developed. With planning and computerization, the colors can make not only stripes but also faux Fair Isle designs, animal print effects, and a variety of other patterns in the finished knit. The result can be so complex that it looks like many yarns were used when, in fact, it was knit with just one yarn. This type of dyeing can be mimicked in hand dyeing, but it is very labor intensive because the skeins are long, sometimes twenty or more feet in length. Because these yarns are purposely designed to make a pattern, they are not included in this book and will not give the same effect as the other variegates when using the techniques described here.

The very long color sections in this yarn will make distinct stripes because the colors contrast greatly and there is no blending between them. The width of the stripes will vary, depending on your gauge and the width of the knit piece.

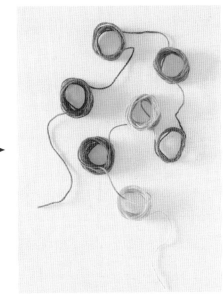

This commercially spun yarn has many colors, and the length of each varies. Some are just a yard long and others are several yards long. This yarn will knit up as stripes of random widths.

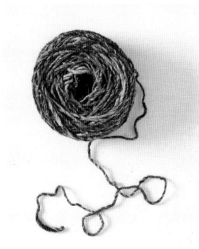

This is a popular, commercially spun yarn from Japan with very long color sections that blend from one to the next. This yarn is created in the same way that hand-spun yarns are made: The fibers are dyed first, then spun one color at a time with just slight blending where they join. This look cannot be achieved by dyeing the yarn after it is spun.

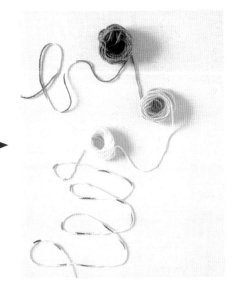

The long sections of pink, white, and fuchsia in this yarn will knit into stripes while the tiny specks of color will give the look of Fair Isle, probably showing up as just a stitch or two in each spot.

Colors in the Skein versus Knitted Colors

Why do knitters love the colors in a variegated skein, but not necessarily like them after they're knitted up? The length of the repeats, both of each color and of the sequence of colors, is what causes colors to flash, pool, or make zigzag designs in a piece of knitting. Color repeats are good and necessary, though, because they make the yarn look the same throughout the skein, as well as throughout the dye lot. Without a consistent repeat, it would be difficult to make the sleeves on a sweater look like they match the sweater's body.

Comparing Gauge Swatches

There's no way to know for certain what pattern the colors may form in your knitting project. Even knitting a swatch won't answer the question entirely, because both the number of stitches used and the gauge affect the patterning. The photos on these pages show examples of the same colorway knit in a four-inch-wide swatch, a ten-inch-wide swatch, and a twenty-inch-wide swatch, all to the same gauge. The smallest swatch is 20 stitches wide, the next is 45 stitches wide, and the largest is 80 stitches wide. Knitting in stockinette stitch (knit one row, purl one row) shows the colors in the same sequence in which they are dyed, so pooling or patterning of some kind is almost guaranteed. Even though knitting a swatch won't tell you what the finished project will look like, swatching

is necessary to obtain gauge. With variegated yarns, it can also help you to see whether the colors will tend to pool or pattern. If the color sections are very short and there are many colors in the skein, it is possible that little or no noticeable pooling will occur. The samples here demonstrate that swatching will not give an accurate prediction of what patterning or pooling will occur, but it does tell you that it will happen. Just the fact that it does occur means that it's a good idea to use one of the techniques or stitch patterns shown in the following chapters to deter pooling. Other variables that will affect the look of the finished project include which type of variegated yarn is used (spotted, or short or long repeats), what stitch pattern is used, and the knitter's own knitting style.

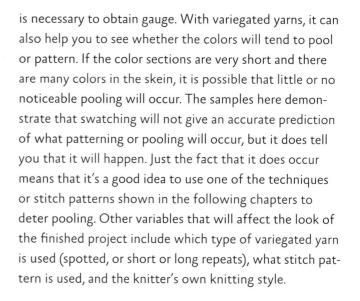

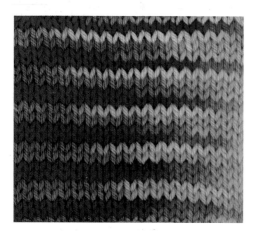

Four-inch-wide swatch: This small swatch appears to have stripes. At this width, one loop of yarn, or repeat, is approximately the right amount of yarn to knit four rows, which allows the colors to stack up on the ends, so two rows form stripes.

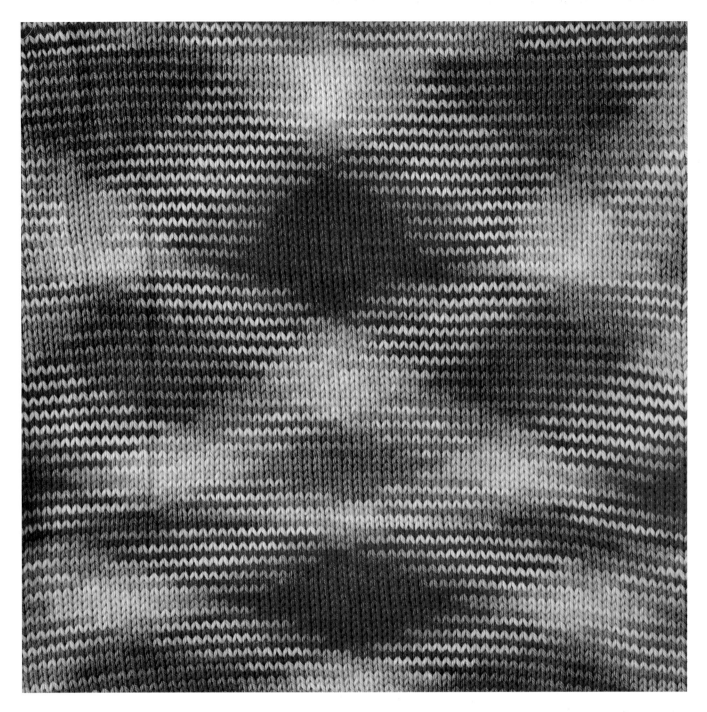

(Left) Ten-inch-wide-swatch: The medium swatch is worked on twice as many stitches so one repeat knits about two rows across. Again, horizontal stripes form, although it is more of a zigzag because the colors stagger by a few stitches each row.

(Above) Twenty-inch-wide-swatch: On the largest swatch, the color repeat doesn't even complete one row of knitting, so the same colors are worked in the following row. The colors don't line up straight, but are staggered every few stitches and the pooling forms diamonds, or an argyle pattern. This is completely unpredictable.

You can see that the diamonds are not consistent all the way through the swatch. Part of the reason for this is that the yarn is hand-dyed so the length of each color varies. The slightest change in gauge will affect the patterning.

Choosing the Right Knitting Technique for Your Colorway

Throughout this book, six colorways are used in the stitch pattern samples in each chapter. Here a stockinette stitch swatch (knit one row, purl one row) of each of the colors shows what the colors look like if no technique or stitch pattern or contrasting color is added. The patterning that shows up is not a prediction of how a project would look but rather an indication that a pattern will form, and to avoid this you can use one of the techniques from the following chapters.

A look at the colors shows that some work better than others for each technique. The type of colorway you're working with—whether calm or active—will play a major role in how its colors look when they're knitted, and which techniques are likely to remedy or minimize those effects. When choosing your variegated colorway, look at the individual colors in the skein. In some colorways the colors flow gently from one to the next and with others there is a clash of colors. Place the yarn about ten feet away from you and squint at it. You may see a fuzzy blend of colors or you may see one color that stands out from the rest. Determining whether the colorway you're using is calm or active is the first thing you need to do because this will affect which technique you choose and its success.

Calm Colorways

A calm colorway is one in which one color blends into the next with no single color making a bold statement. A calm colorway may be monochromatic; that is, it may be formed from many gentle shades of one color, like the mauve, pink, lavender colorway (below, left). Colorways in which all the colors are similar in intensity can also be called calm. The earth tones (below, center) all share the attention equally; there isn't one color that stands out from the rest. A calm colorway can also look like a watercolor painting, where the colors blend and soak into each other gently without any harsh edges, sometimes making it hard to tell where one color ends and the next one begins. The dark rainbow colorway (below, right) is an example of this. When these colors are knit, even in stockinette, they may pool or pattern, but the colors are gentle and flowing and the pooling will be subtle and understated. Compare these swatches to those in each chapter when considering which technique to use.

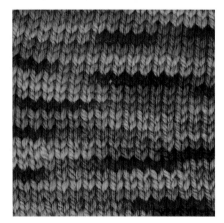

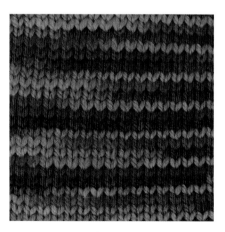

This colorway of pinks and lavenders has very similar shades of one color throughout. It is monochromatic or tone on tone.

This colorway has many colors in it, but they all are equal in brightness and intensity. No single color jumps out from the rest, so these are balanced colors.

This colorway qualifies as being a balanced color but it also creates the illusion that one color fades and blends into the next, like watercolors.

Active Colorways

Active colorways are the opposite of calm ones. In these yarns, each color fights for dominance as the yarn switches from one color to another, and there's a lot of contrast between the colors. They may be bright, intense, or have strong dark-to-light contrast. The colors appear to actively move from light to dark or pale to bright.

The colorway (below, left) that jumps from fuchsia to brown with tan and green in between has a very high contrast between colors and between the brightness of those colors. It can be a challenge to work with yarns like this because the colors all compete for attention. Although the blue, teal, and turquoise colorway (below, center) is monochromatic, the difference between the light and dark colors is very strong, making it active. The bright rainbow colorway (below, right) keeps your eye jumping from one color to another, definitely an active colorway. Compare the swatches below to those in each chapter when considering a particular technique.

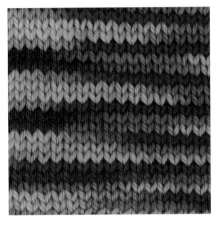

This colorway has light and dark, bright and muted colors. In some way every color vies for attention. When two or more colors are strong and stand out from the rest, they are what I call the zingers.

This colorway is shades of one color, but the contrast between the shades is great. The difference between the light aqua and the dark turquoise is distinct, so think of it as shadows of one color.

The colors in this yarn are all equally bright and bold, and with little or no blending between the colors. Since all the colors are strong, they all crave attention equally. This is known as a rainbow pattern.

Evaluating Your Yarn

Yarns come packaged in skeins, reeled in hanks, rolled into balls, flattened into pancakes, and swirled into center-pull skeins. How do you identify which type of dyeing technique was used for the yarn and how do you know what to expect from the skein before you buy it?

Most hand-dyed yarns come in a loosely wound skein or hank, a large circle that is tied in several places to prevent tangling. If the colors on this hank are in defined sections, then the skein is exactly as it came from the dye pots. This is the easiest yarn to identify. Look at the colors to see if a color is repeated or if it's dyed in only one place. If a color is in more than one place or is a longer section than the other colors, it will dominate and probably cause pooling. You can see how much of each color is used and what the repeat is. You can see whether the color repeat makes a full circle or whether the skein was folded prior to dyeing, which would make the colors reverse order halfway around the circle. These are all helpful details to recognize, and each of the following chapters gives different techniques and suggestions on how to use these yarns.

If the yarn is in a pull skein or a commercially wound skein, or if a hank has been rewound to jumble the colors, it's harder to identify its color information. Ask the yarn shop owner how long the color sections are in the pull skeins. Some yarn labels will say "self-striping" or "self-patterning"; others may have a model knit that shows how long the colors run. If it's a yarn that you already own, you can unwind about two yards and lay it on a flat surface. See if the colors repeat in such a way that you can form a circle and have the colors line up. This is more likely to happen with hand-dyed than with commercial yarns, but with either type it is helpful to observe how long the color sections are and if there is a repeat. Note whether the color is tiny dots, or short or long sections. Identifying whether the colors are spotted, or in short or long sections, will give you an idea of how likely it is to pool and what type of technique you might use to prevent the yarn from pooling.

This is a skein of hand-dyed wool. It is packaged in an old-fashioned center-pull skein, which could give the impression that it is commercially dyed. By unwinding a few yards and rewinding them so that the colors line up, it's easy to see where the color repeat is, how long the color sections are, and how much of each color there is in proportion to the other colors.

How to Use the Stitch Patterns

Each of the following chapters presents a different knitting technique, illustrated by four to six stitch patterns, each of which is knit in one of the six colorways shown on pages 20–21. A brief description of each swatch explains what types of variegated yarn would work well with it, and the kind of project the stitch pattern would best lend itself to.

As shown below, each stitch pattern is presented in written instructions and, where helpful, as a chart. There is a stitch repeat given for each one. If the stitch repeat is for three stitches, then simply cast on a multiple of 3, whether it's 30 stitches to make a scarf or 90 stitches to make a blanket. If the repeat is 3 plus 2, use a number that is a multiple of 3 (such as 30 or 90), but then add 2 to the end, making it 32 or 92. (This is usually done to center a pattern or keep the edges symmetrical.) Most stitch patterns can be inserted into any simple pattern, as long as you knit a swatch first to get the same gauge as the pattern.

To follow a chart, read right-side rows from right to left and wrong-side rows from left to right. Each square on the chart represents one stitch and the key explains what each symbol means. Oftentimes, a chart helps you to see how the stitches align and makes the pattern fall into place more logically.

Each chapter also includes two projects—one simple and the other more complex—that use the featured technique. Each project uses one of the stitch patterns in the chapter. There are four more stitch patterns or swatches that show a similar stitch pattern or technique for you to try. Once you have compared your colorway to those shown in the chapters, you will have a better idea as to which technique and which stitch patterns will work best with your yarn choice. Use these stitch patterns and techniques to make your own colorway look fantastic!

Pleasing Plaid Stitch (multiple of 3)

This stitch pattern is easy to work and can be used in many projects because of the small stitch repeat. Another variation, not shown here, is to work Rows 1 and 2 in a solid and Rows 3 and 4 in variegated. The change in appearance is dramatic.

Row 1 and 3 (RS): K1, *sl 1 as if to purl wyib, k2; repeat from * to last two stitches, sl 1 as if to purl wyib, k1.

Row 2: P1, *sl 1 as if to purl wyif, p2; repeat from * to last two stitches, sl 1 as if to purl wyif, p1.

Row 4: P1, knit to last stitch, p1.

Repeat Rows 1–4 for pattern.

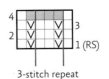

3-stitch repeat

☐ k on RS, p on WS
▨ p on RS, k on WS
☑ sl 1 as if to purl with yarn on WS

chapter

two

MAKING TWO LOOK LIKE ONE

Blending Mismatched Skeins

When choosing hand-dyed yarns for a project, it's important to remember that the yarn is in fact "hand" dyed, that is, dyed by a person, not by a computerized machine that precisely places the dye onto the yarn. Even skeins within the same dye lot may vary. The amount that the skeins vary is different, depending on the company. Some companies are known for having very consistent colors and dye lots, while others actually take pride in the fact that each of their skeins is distinctive or artistic. Even skeins that look alike before they're knitted may actually knit up a little differently. If a stripe or swirling pattern forms with one skein, there's no guarantee that the next skein will continue that pattern. Commercially dyed or printed yarns will have more consistency, in terms of the colors and length of each color, however the pattern could still change based solely on where in the color repeat the new ball is joined. If a diamond or argyle is forming, you'll want to join the new yarn in the precise sequence of colors that's been established. On the following pages are several simple ways to make sure that an entire project will have continuity of colors and that where one skein ends and the next begins won't be obvious. All the swatches in this chapter are knit in stockinette stitch (knit one row, purl one row) to make it easier to see the color changes.

Double Stranding

You can use two strands of hand-dyed yarn together, treating them as one single, thicker yarn. Naturally, this completely changes the gauge. The new, thicker yarn that you have created can be knitted in any pattern that calls for a single yarn with a similar gauge. This opens up all kinds of possibilities for using finer yarns that, when doubled, will knit up more quickly. Two strands of sock yarn will knit up at about the same gauge as a worsted-weight yarn.

Using two identical yarns will mix up the colors because the colors on each strand are not likely to match up in the same places; they will shift and blend between the two skeins, making an even mix of all the colors. In the swatch using two strands of variegated yarn (right, top), notice how the same colors rarely match up in each stitch. Instead, each stitch contains two or more colors. This technique works in many variations. The two yarns can be the same variegated colorway or one can be a solid (right, bottom). Choosing a solid color for the second yarn impacts on the color scheme. With the rainbow-colored yarn, for example, there are many options. Stranding purple with this colorway, as shown here, makes the overall look purple with flashes of yellow, red, and green.

Both strands don't necessarily have to be the same yarn. They can be different weights or even different textures. One could be a hand-dyed sportweight yarn, and the other a solid sock-weight yarn. Try mixing a solid laceweight mohair with a sportweight variegated yarn. Or knit together a variegated sock yarn with another variegated laceweight yarn. Mixing them will soften and blend the colors together and keep the colors consistent throughout the project. There are many options for creating your own yarn and color mixes.

Double Stranding in Stockinette Stitch

Holding two strands of yarn together throughout, knit right-side rows and purl wrong-side rows.

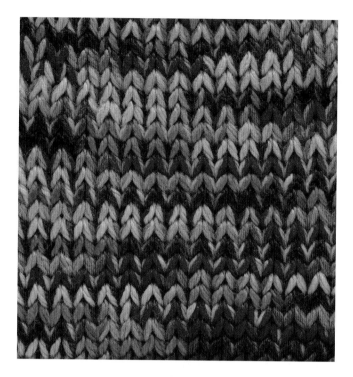

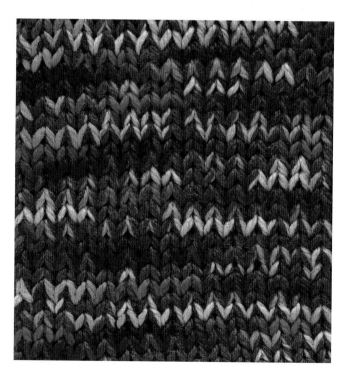

Alternating Skeins

By knitting alternate rows with two different skeins, the sequence of the colors is broken. One skein may form one repetitive pattern, and the second yarn may form another pattern, but when the yarn is alternated in rows, the patterns are shuffled. The simplest way to do this is to knit two rows from one skein, then knit two rows from the other skein, throughout the project, as shown in the swatch at right. If you're knitting in the round, you can switch yarns more frequently or less so, every other round or every third round—it's up to you. If a project is expected to use three skeins of yarn, you can work back and forth in single rows with each of the three skeins. One yarn will always be ready and waiting for the next row. The resulting swatch will be a good overall blend of the colors.

With this technique, if the colors from each skein should stack or otherwise form a pattern, cut one yarn and start knitting with it in a different place, or knit with it from the other end of the skein. This method is particularly successful with colorways that are one way, where the colors are in one order from one end of the skein and reverse order from the other end of the skein. With a one-way colorway, be sure to work from opposite ends when alternating rows.

Alternating Double Rows from Two Skeins in Stockinette Stitch

Use two skeins of the same yarn, carrying unused yarn along the edge.
Row 1 (RS): With first end, knit.
Row 2: With first yarn end, purl.
Row 3: With second yarn end, knit.
Row 4: With second yarn end, purl.

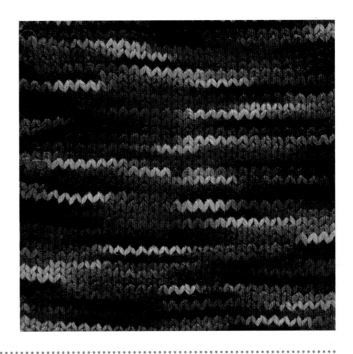

Different Sections, Different Skeins

Using different skeins for distinct sections of a project highlights the variations in the skeins. Some parts of a project—for example, the edging on a sweater, or a hood or collar—are meant to look different from the rest. One way to emphasize this is to use one skein exclusively for those elements. You can also use a different skein for sections in a project that are knit in a different direction, such as diagonal or mitered squares. In the swatch at right, the upper part is long and narrow, which makes the colors form an entirely different pattern than the wider lower part; this looks exactly the same as the regular stockinette swatch. The top part has wide stripes, which show the colors very clearly, because the length of each color in the yarn is nearly the same as the width of the knitting. This technique is especially interesting when the two sections are worked with a very different number of stitches. The stripes or patterns that form look like they were intentionally knit that way.

Multidirectional Elements in Stockinette Stitch

Cast on 9 stitches. Work in stockinette stitch for 4". Bind off. Pick up and knit along the side edge approximately three stitches for every four rows. Work in stockinette for 3". Bind off.

ENGLISH ROSE TUNIC

Each of the skeins of this hand-dyed yarn looked a little different from the other. Some had more green; some had more pink. By double stranding, the different-colored skeins are blended throughout. Since the yarn is a fine weight, knitting with two strands also gives the garment more body.

SKILL LEVEL
Intermediate

SIZES
Woman's Extra Small (Small, Medium, Large, Extra Large) *Instructions are for smallest size, with changes for other sizes noted in parentheses as necessary.*

FINISHED MEASUREMENTS
Bust: 36 (40, 44, 48, 52)"

MATERIALS
- Farmhouse Wool Silk Blend (34% silk, 33% wool, 33% cotton; 4 oz/113g, 350 yds/320m): 6 (7, 8, 8, 9) skeins in Rose Garden
- Size 9 (5.5mm) straight needles
- Size 9 (5.5mm) 16" circular needle
- 5 stitch holders
- Five ¾" buttons (shown here: JHB Fleur de corozo #30247 in rose)
- Tapestry needle

GAUGE
16 stitches and 20 rows = 4" in stockinette stictch using double strand throughout

STITCH PATTERN
Double Stranding in Stockinette Stitch
Holding two strands of yarn together throughout, knit right-side rows and purl wrong-side rows.

NOTES
The upper body is knit first. After overlapping the front pieces, the lower body is picked up and knit downward, making it easy to adjust for length or to see how your yarn supply lasts. Once front and back are finished and joined at the shoulders, the sleeves are picked up and knit downward, using short rows for the cap sleeves.

BACK YOKE

With straight needles, cast on 72 (80, 88, 96, 104) stitches, knit two rows to make a ridge on the right side. Begin stockinette stitch. Work even until yoke measures 4", ending with a wrong side row.

Shape Armholes

At beginning of next two rows, bind off 5 (6, 7, 6, 8) stitches for underarm. Decrease one stitch on each edge every right-side row 4 (5, 5, 6, 7) times—54 (58, 64, 72, 74) stitches. Work even in stockinette stitch until armhole measures 8 (8 ½, 9, 9 ½, 10)". Place 14 (16, 18, 20, 20) stitches on each end on separate holders for shoulders. Place center 26 (26, 28, 32, 34) stitches on holder for back neck.

LOWER BACK

Turn yoke upside down. With straight needles and right side facing, pick up stitches along cast-on edge, leaving one garter ridge showing. Pick up and knit 72 (80, 88, 96, 104) stitches. Work even in stockinette stitch until lower back measures 14 (15, 15 ½, 16 ½, 17)". Begin working 4 stitches at each edge in garter stitch. When lower section measures 17 (18, 18 ½, 19 ½, 20)", change to garter stitch across all stitches. Work even for ½". Bind off all stitches.

LEFT FRONT YOKE

With straight needles, cast on 40 (44, 48, 52, 56) stitches. Knit two rows to make a ridge on the right side. Keep 4 stitches at left edge in garter stitch while working remainder in stockinette stitch. Work even until yoke measures 4", ending with a wrong-side row.

Shape Armhole

At beginning of next right-side row, bind off 5 (6, 7, 6, 8) stitches for underarm. Decrease one stitch on right edge every right-side row 4 (5, 5, 6, 7) times—31 (33, 36, 40, 41) stitches. Work even as established until armhole measures 5 (5 ½, 6, 6 ½, 7)", ending with a right-side row.

Shape Neck

At beginning of next wrong-side row, bind off 8 stitches for neck. Bind off 3 stitches at beginning of every wrong-side row 3 (3, 2, 4, 3) times, then bind off two stitches at beginning of every wrong-side row 0 (0, 2, 0, 2) times. Work even on 14 (16, 18, 20, 20) stitches until the front measures same as the back to shoulders. Place on holder for shoulders.

RIGHT FRONT YOKE

With straight needles, cast on 40 (44, 48, 52, 56) stitches. Knit two rows to make a ridge on the right side. Keep 4 stitches at the right edge in garter stitch while working the remainder in stockinette stitch. When yoke measures 1½", work buttonhole on the next right-side row as follows: K2, yo, k2tog, knit to end. Work three more buttonholes every 2 (2, 2 ½, 2 ½, 2 ½)". When yoke measures 4", shape armhole.

Shape Armhole

At beginning of next wrong-side row, bind off 5 (6, 7, 6, 8) stitches for underarm. Decrease one stitch on right edge every right-side row 4 (5, 5, 6, 7) times—31 (33, 38, 40, 41) stitches. Work even as established until armhole measures 5 (5 ½, 6, 6 ½, 7)", ending with a wrong-side row.

Shape Neck

At beginning of next right-side row, bind off 8 stitches for neck. Bind off 3 stitches at beginning of every right-side row 3 (3, 2, 4, 3) times, then bind off two stitches at beginning of every right-side row 0 (0, 2, 0, 2) times. Work even on 14 (16, 18, 20, 20) stitches until the front measures the same as the back to shoulders. Place on holder for shoulders.

With right sides together, join fronts to back at shoulders, using the **three-needle bind-off** as follows: Hold the two pieces of knitting with the needles parallel in your left hand. With a third needle, knit the first stitch on both needles together and move it to the right needle. Knit the second stitch on each needle, and pass the first stitch over the second. Continue in this way across until all your stitches are bound off.

Sew buttons to the Left Front opposite the buttonholes, then overlap and button fronts together. Pick up and knit stitches from the lower edge same as for the lower back, but pick up through both layers where the four stitches overlap.

Work Lower Front the same as for Lower Back.

SLEEVES

With circular needles, beginning at center of underarm, pick up and knit 52 (56, 60, 64, 68) stitches around armhole, including 10 (12, 14, 12, 16) stitches from stitches previously bound off. Break yarn. Slip 19 (21, 23, 24, 26) stitches. Join yarn. Purl 14 (14, 14, 16, 16) stitches, turn work. Slip 1, k14 (14, 14, 16, 16), turn work. Slip 1, p15 (15, 15, 17, 17), turn work. Continue to slip the first stitch and work one more stitch than previous row every row until 5 (6, 7, 6, 8) stitches remain at each end. For last two rows work across all stitches.

Continue to work in stockinette stitch, decreasing one stitch at each edge every eighth row 7 (8, 10, 10, 11) times. Work even on 38 (40, 40, 44, 46) stitches until sleeve measures 16 (17, 17 ½, 18, 18 ½)" from underarm or ½" shorter than desired length. Change to garter stitch for ½". Bind off.

NECK EDGING

Using circular needle, with right side facing pick up and knit approximately 68 (68, 72, 76, 80) stitches around neck edge. Knit one row. Work buttonhole on next row same as previous buttonholes, knit to end of row. Knit one row more. Bind off all stitches.

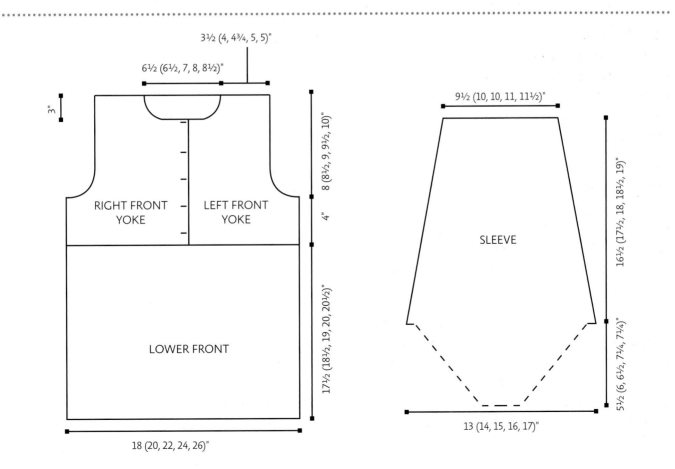

SHADES OF DAWN MITERED SHAWL

Each square of this shawl could be worked without changing yarns but, since the colors vary from skein to skein (and from dye lot to dye lot), each square would look slightly different from the other squares. By alternating skeins, working a few inches from one ball of yarn, then a few inches from another ball for each square, the shawl is consistent in color.

SKILL LEVEL
Easy

SIZES
One Size

FINISHED MEASUREMENTS
36" square

MATERIALS
- Fiesta Yarns Baby Boom (100% extrafine superwash merino; 2 oz/57g, 220 yds/201m): 5 skeins (numbered 1, 2, 3, 4, and 5) in Sandstone
- Size 4 (3.5 mm) needles
- Removable stitch marker

GAUGE
5 stitches and 10 rows = 1" in Lace Stitch Pattern on size 4 needles

LACE STITCH PATTERN
Row 1 (right side): Slip 1 as if to purl wyif, *yo, k2tog; repeat from * to two stitches before marked stitch, slip 2 tog as if to knit, k1, pass two slipped stitches over, *k2tog, yo; repeat from * to last stitch, k1.

Row 2 and all wrong side rows: Slip 1, as if to purl wyib, knit to marker, p1, knit to end.

Row 3: Slip 1 as if to purl wyif, knit to two stitches before marked stitch, slip 2 tog as if to knit, k1, pass two slipped stitches over, knit to end.

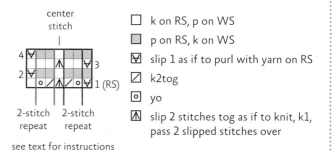

center stitch

	k on RS, p on WS
	p on RS, k on WS
	slip 1 as if to purl with yarn on RS
	k2tog
	yo
	slip 2 stitches tog as if to knit, k1, pass 2 slipped stitches over

2-stitch repeat   2-stitch repeat

see text for instructions

NOTES
The center square is knit first from the wide edge to the center point, from the bottom two edges of the diamond to the top center point. As decreases are worked at the center, the diamond is formed. Each side square is picked up and knit from this one.

In order to blend all the skeins evenly throughout, each square is worked with all five skeins. Change skeins in the same sequence, working a specific number of rows as written, or, if you have a scale, work eighteen grams of each skein before changing to the next skein.

CENTER SQUARE

Using Skein 1, cast on 181 stitches. Place marker through center stitch. Knit one row. Begin lace pattern. Work for 16 rows (8 ridges). Change to Skein 2, continue in pattern for 20 rows (total 18 ridges). Change to Skein 3, continue in pattern for 24 rows (total 30 ridges). Change to Skein 4, continue in pattern for 28 rows (total 44 ridges). Change to Skein 5, continue until 3 stitches remain. K3tog, finish off. Cut yarn.

RIGHT SQUARE

Using Skein 1, cast on 90 stitches, pick up and knit one stitch from far right corner of center square, place marker through it, pick up and knit 90 stitches along right edge of center square—181 stitches. If it is difficult to pick up enough stitches, pick up one stitch per ridge, then increase evenly on next row to make 90 stitches. Knit one row. Work in pattern same as for center square.

LEFT SQUARE

Using Skein 1, pick up and knit 90 stitches along left edge of the center square (see tip on right square), pick up and knit one stitch at far left corner of center square, place marker through it, cast on 90 stitches—181 stitches. Knit one row. Work in pattern same as for center square. Block to measurements and to show lace pattern.

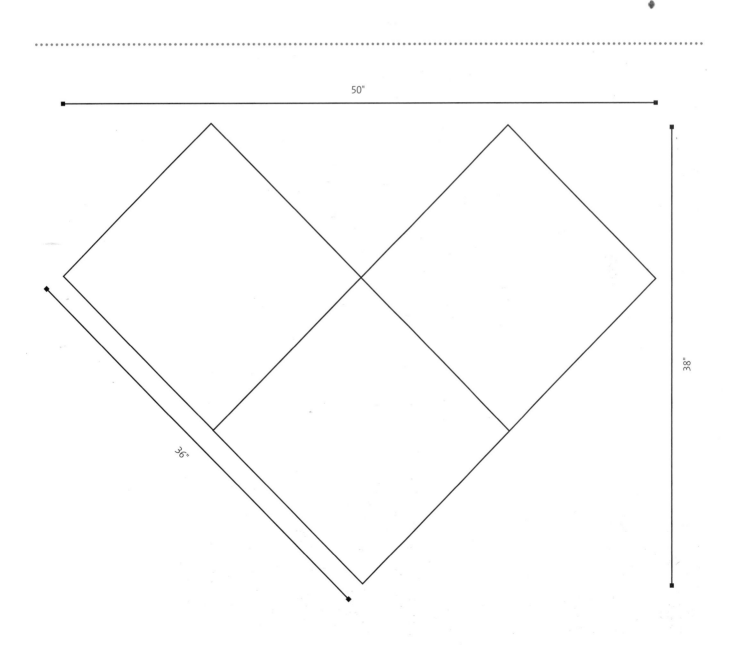

chapter

three

A LITTLE TEXTURE GOES A LONG WAY

Knits and Purls, Cables, Bobbles, and Other Textures

Sometimes using a textured stitch is just enough to mix up the colors in a variegated project. Adding texture allows the colors of your skein to be the focal point while keeping them blended and preventing patterning. Smooth yarns worked in a stitch pattern that adds bumps or ripples to the fabric helps prevent pooling of the colors. The techniques in this chapter include knitting stitches together in bobbles or bunches, working cables or purl stitches on a background of stockinette, and working allover stitch patterns.

Knits and Purls

The more texture you add to a knit fabric, the more it breaks up the color changes in the yarn. Stitch patterns that make vertical and horizontal ribs are great at mixing up colors because the yarn from the previous row mixes, with the current row whenever a purl stitch is worked-mixing the colors from two rows.

Angled Rib Stitch (multiple of 10)

Row 1 (RS): *P6, (k1, p1) 2 times; repeat from * across.
Row 2 and all WS rows: Knit the knit stitches and purl the purl stitches.
Row 3: *K7, p1, k1, p1; repeat from * across.
Row 5: *K1, p7, k1, p1; repeat from * across.
Row 7: *K1, p1, k7, p1; repeat from * across.
Row 9: *K1, p1, k1, p7; repeat from * across.
Row 11: *(K1, p1) 2 times, k6; repeat from * across.
Row 13: *P2, k1, p1, k1, p5; repeat from * across.
Row 15: *K3, p1, k1, p1, k4; repeat from * across.
Row 17: *P4, k1, p1, k1, p3; repeat from * across.
Row 19: *K5, p1, k1, p1, k2; repeat from * across.
Row 20: *P2, k1, p1, k1, p5; repeat from * across.
Repeat Rows 1–20 for pattern.

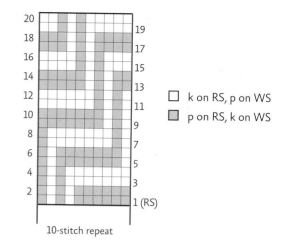

☐ k on RS, p on WS
▨ p on RS, k on WS

10-stitch repeat

....

Bobbles and Bunches

A bobble, a small bubble on the right side of the work, is made by increasing into the stitch, working those stitches back and forth, decreasing them back down to one stitch, then continuing across the row. When working a bobble, be sure to keep the stitches snug at the finishing end. Bobbles can be very small (page 39, right), increasing just a few stitches and working a couple of rows back and forth, or they can be very large, increasing several times, knitting many rows, then decreasing back down. A large bobble can even be stuffed or knit in a different color. You can vary a bobble pattern by spacing the bobbles closer together or farther apart. Similar stitches, such as the bramble stitch (page 39, left), sometimes known as the trinity stitch because three stitches are worked out of one, gather and bunch stitches together and also mix the colors well. Bobble and bunch patterns are bulky and add dimension to the knitting so they are best used in one area of a project, such as the sleeves, or for small projects like hats, pillows, or purses.

Bramble Stitch (multiple of 4)

Row 1 (WS): *(K1, yo, k1) in same stitch, p3tog; repeat from * across.

Row 2: *P1, k3; repeat from * across.

Row 3: *P3tog, (k1, yo, k1) in same stitch; repeat from * across.

Row 4: *K3, p1; repeat from * across.

Repeat Rows 1–4 for pattern.

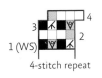

4-stitch repeat

☐ k on RS, p on WS

▨ p on RS, k on WS

◩ p3tog on WS

▽ (k1, yo, k1) in one stitch on WS

■ no stitch

Mini Bobbles Stitch (multiple of 6 + 2)

Bobble: (K1, yo, k1) into next stitch, turn, p3, turn, slip 1, k2tog, pass slipped stitch over.

Row 1 (RS): Knit.

Row 2 and all WS rows: Purl.

Row 3: *K2, bobble, k3; repeat from * to last two stitches, k2.

Row 5: Knit.

Row 7: *K5, bobble; repeat from * to last two stitches, k2.

Row 8: Purl.

Repeat Rows 1–8 for pattern.

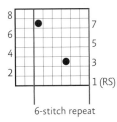

6-stitch repeat

☐ k on RS, p on WS

◉ bobble

Cables

Cables are much simpler than they appear at first. A cable is made by slipping one or more stitches onto a small cable needle and holding that needle in front or back of the work while working the next stitch or stitches on the left needle, then returning to the cable needle and knitting those stitches. The pattern will always tell you how many stitches to hold and whether to hold them in front or back of your work. Using cables with hand-dyed yarns changes the order of the colors every time a cable is crossed so the colors will be mixed up and not form patterns. The chicken wire cable (right) is worked only over three stitches, but on the cabled Rows 5 and 11, every stitch is displaced, moving the color sequence and preventing pooling. Cables can be spaced out or worked over the entire fabric. Even a small cable of just two stitches, also called a traveling stitch (page 41, left), will change the order of the yarn colors within the row. You can use these stitch patterns for an entire garment or for a center panel on a sweater or blanket.

Chicken Wire Cable (multiple of 6 + 2)

1/2 RPC: Slip next two stitches onto cable needle and hold in back, p1, k2 from cable needle.

1/2 LPC: Slip next stitch onto cable needle and hold in front, k2, p1 from cable needle.

Rows 1 and 3 (RS): P3, *k2, p4; repeat from * to last five stitches, k2, p3.

Rows 2 and 4: K3, *p2, k4; repeat from * to last five stitches, p2, k3.

Row 5: P1, *1/2 RPC, 1/2 LPC; repeat from * to last stitch, p1.

Rows 6, 8, and 10: K1, p1, *k4, p2; repeat from * to last six stitches, k4, p1, k1.

Rows 7 and 9: P1, k1, *p4, k2; repeat from * to last 6 stitches, p4, k1, p1.

Row 11: P1, *1/2 LPC, 1/2 RPC; repeat from * to last stitch, p1.

Row 12: Same as Row 2.

Repeat Rows 1–12 for pattern.

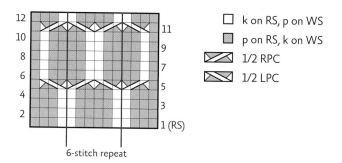

6-stitch repeat

☐ k on RS, p on WS
▨ p on RS, k on WS
◩ 1/2 RPC
◪ 1/2 LPC

Traveling Stitch (multiple of 3)

1/1 LPC: Slip next stitch onto cable needle and hold front, p1, k1 from cable needle.

1/1 RPC: Slip next stitch onto cable needle and hold back, k1, p1 from cable needle.

Rows 1 and 11 (WS): *P1, k2; repeat from * across.

Row 2: *P1, 1/1 RPC; repeat from * across.

Row 3 and 9: *K1, p1, k1; repeat from * across.

Row 4: *1/1 RPC, p1; repeat from * across.

Rows 5 and 7: *K2, p1; repeat from * across.

Row 6: *K1, p2; repeat from * across.

Row 8: *1/1 LPC, p1; repeat from * across.

Row 10: *P1, 1/1 LPC; repeat from * across.

Row 12: *P2, k1; repeat from * across.

Repeat Rows 1–12 for pattern.

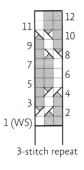

				k on RS, p on WS
				p on RS, k on WS
				1/1 LPC
				1/1 RPC

3-stitch repeat

Purl One Color

If your hand-dyed colorway has very distinctive color changes, you can use this to your advantage by making one of the colors stand out. To do this, you work in stockinette stitch with the exception of the one color you have chosen. When you see that color coming to the needle tip, you work it in reverse stockinette stitch. It may be just a few stitches or it may be many stitches. This stitch pattern doesn't alleviate pooling or patterning of a color but makes it look prettier. The same yarn colorway will look entirely different, depending on which color you focus on, so be sure to swatch it a few ways to see which color choice you like better.

Purl the Pink Stitch (any number of stitches)

Cast on any number of stitches. Work in stockinette stitch (knit on the right side, purl on the wrong side) with one exception: Choose one color—here it's the hot pink—and work it in reverse stockinette stitch (purl on the right side, knit on the wrong side). Whenever that color is ready to be wrapped around the needle, work it in the opposite stitch from the rest of the piece. Do not pay attention to the color of the stitches already on the needles, just to the color of the yarn about to be worked.

BOBBLY BLUE-GREEN MITTENS

Tiny bobbles are used for these mittens—larger bobbles might be a bit overwhelming—and they are worked on the back of the hand only to keep the mittens practical as well as fun. The bobbles mix up the order of the colors in this yarn.

SKILL LEVEL
Intermediate

SIZE
Women's Medium

FINISHED MEASUREMENTS
8" circumference
12" length from cuff to fingertip

MATERIALS
- Hand Painted Knitting Yarns Merino Flecks Worsted Weight 4 MEDIUM (90% fine merino wool, 10% rayon flecks; 3 ½ oz/100g, 170 yds/155 m): 1 skein in Tannhauser
- Set of four size 7 (4.5mm) double-pointed needles
- 3 stitch markers
- Tapestry needle

GAUGE
16 stitches and 20 rounds = 4" in Bobble Stitch Pattern

BOBBLE STITCH PATTERN (multiple of 6 + 3)
Rounds 1–3: Knit.
Round 4: K1, *bobble, k5; repeat from * to last two stitches, bobble, k1.
Rounds 5–7: Knit.
Round 8: K1, *k3, bobble, k2; repeat from * to last two stitches, k2.
Repeat Rounds 1–8 for pattern.

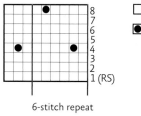

☐ k on RS, p on WS
⬤ bobble

6-stitch repeat

NOTES
Bobbles are worked on the back side of the hand only; the palms are stockinette stitch.
Kfb = Knit into the front and back of the next stitch
Bobble = (K1, yo, k1) into the next stitch, turn, p3, turn, slip 1, k2tog, pass slipped stitch over
Ssk = Slip the first and second stitches knitwise, one at a time, then insert the tip of left-hand needle into the fronts of these two stitches from the left, and knit them together from this position

RIGHT MITTEN

Cast on 30 stitches. Divide stitches evenly on needles. Place marker for beginning of round. Join, being careful not to twist.

Establish ribbing: *K1, p1; repeat from * around. Continue in ribbing for 3".

Rounds 1–3: Knit.

Round 4: Work bobble stitch pattern over 15 stitches, place marker, kfb, k1, kfb, place marker, k12—32 stitches.

Rounds 5–7: Knit.

Round 8: Work bobble stitch pattern over 15 stitches, slip marker, kfb, k3, kfb, slip marker, k12—34 stitches. Continue to increase one stitch inside each marker every fourth round until there are 13 stitches between markers, ending with 2 knit rounds—40 stitches.

Divide for thumb: Work bobble stitch pattern over 15 stitches, remove marker, k2, slip next 10 stitches onto holder for thumb, k13, removing markers—30 stitches.

Hand: Work bobble stitch pattern over 15 stitches, k15. Continue in established pattern until hand measures 3¾" from thumb opening.

Shape Top

Round 1: K1, ssk, work established bobble stitch pattern over 9 stitches, k2tog, k2, ssk, k9, k2tog, k1—26 stitches.

Round 2: K2, work bobble stitch pattern over 9 stitches, knit to end.

Round 3: K1, ssk, work bobble stitch pattern over 7 stitches, k2tog, k2, ssk, k7, k2tog, k1—22 stitches.

Round 4: K2, work bobble stitch pattern over 7 stitches, knit to end.

Round 5: K1, ssk, work bobble stitch pattern over 5 stitches, k2tog, k2, ssk, k5, k2tog, k1—18 stitches.

Round 6: K2, work bobble stitch pattern over 5 stitches, knit to end.

Round 7: K1, ssk, work bobble stitch pattern over 3 stitches, k2tog, k2, ssk, k3, k2tog, k1—14 stitches.

Round 8: K2, work bobble stitch pattern over 3 stitches, knit to end.

Cut yarn, leaving an 18" tail. Divide stitches evenly onto two needles. Using tapestry needle, graft stitches together using **kitchener stitch**, as follows:

With the working yarn in back, insert the tapestry needle through the first stitch on the front needle as if to knit, and drop it off the needle. Insert the needle through the second stitch, as if to purl and leave it on the needle.

Insert the tapestry needle through the first stitch on the back needle as if to purl, and drop it off the needle. Insert the needle through the second stitch as if to knit, and leave it on the needle. Tighten the yarn. Repeat these four steps.

Thumb: Place 10 stitches from holder onto two needles; with a third needle, pick up and knit 4 stitches from cast-on edge—14 stitches. Knit every round until thumb measures 1½".

Next round: (K2tog) around. Knit one round. Cut yarn, leaving a 6" tail. Using tapestry needle, thread tail through remaining stitches twice. Pull tight and fasten off yarn. Weave in ends.

LEFT MITTEN

Work ribbing same as for right mitten.

Rounds 1–3: Knit.

Round 4: Work bobble stitch pattern over 15 stitches, k12, place marker, kfb, k1, kfb—32 stitches.

Rounds 5–7: Knit.

Round 8: Work bobble stitch pattern over 15 stitches, k12, slip marker, kfb, k3, kfb—34 stitches. Continue to increase one stitch inside each marker every fourth round until there are 13 stitches between markers, ending with 2 knit rounds—40 stitches.

Divide for thumb: Work bobble stitch pattern over 15 stitches, k13, remove marker, slip next 10 stitches to holder for thumb, k2—30 stitches.

Complete hand, top shaping, and thumb as for right mitten.

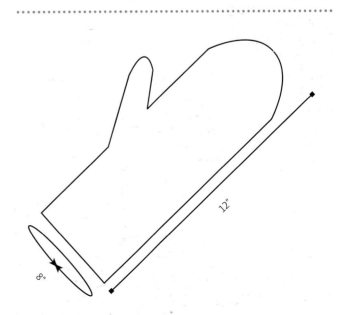

PRIMARY SCHOOL CARDIGAN

Purling one color is fun and easy, and it accentuates one of the colors—which one is your choice. However, colors can still pool, leaving all the purl bumps in one section of the garment. So use the technique of working from two skeins when you purl one color.

SKILL LEVEL
Easy

SIZES
Child Sizes 4 (6, 8, 10) *Instructions are for smallest size, with changes for other sizes noted in parentheses as necessary.*

FINISHED MEASUREMENTS
Chest sizes: 28 (30, 32, 34)"

MATERIALS
- Prism Custom Dyed Yarns Symphony **3 LIGHT** (80% merino, 10% cashmere, 10% nylon; 2 oz/57g, 118 yds/108m): 7 (8, 9, 11) skeins in Cantina
- Size 4 (3.5mm) needles
- 4 stitch markers
- Scrap yarn for holders
- Tapestry needle
- Six ¾" buttons (shown here: JHB #53498 "Stop" and "Go" buttons)

GAUGE
20 stitches and 34 rows = 1" in stitch pattern on size 4 needles

STITCH PATTERN
Sweater is worked in stockinette stitch (knit right-side rows, purl wrong-side rows), with this exception: Whenever purple (or your chosen color) approaches the needle, that color is worked in reverse stockinette stitch (purl right-side rows, knit wrong-side rows). Ignore the color of the stitches on the needle; only pay attention to the color of the yarn that is about to be knit.

NOTES
The front button and buttonhole bands are incorporated into the fronts. Back and fronts are knit in three pieces then joined at the shoulders. Sleeves are picked up and knit downward.

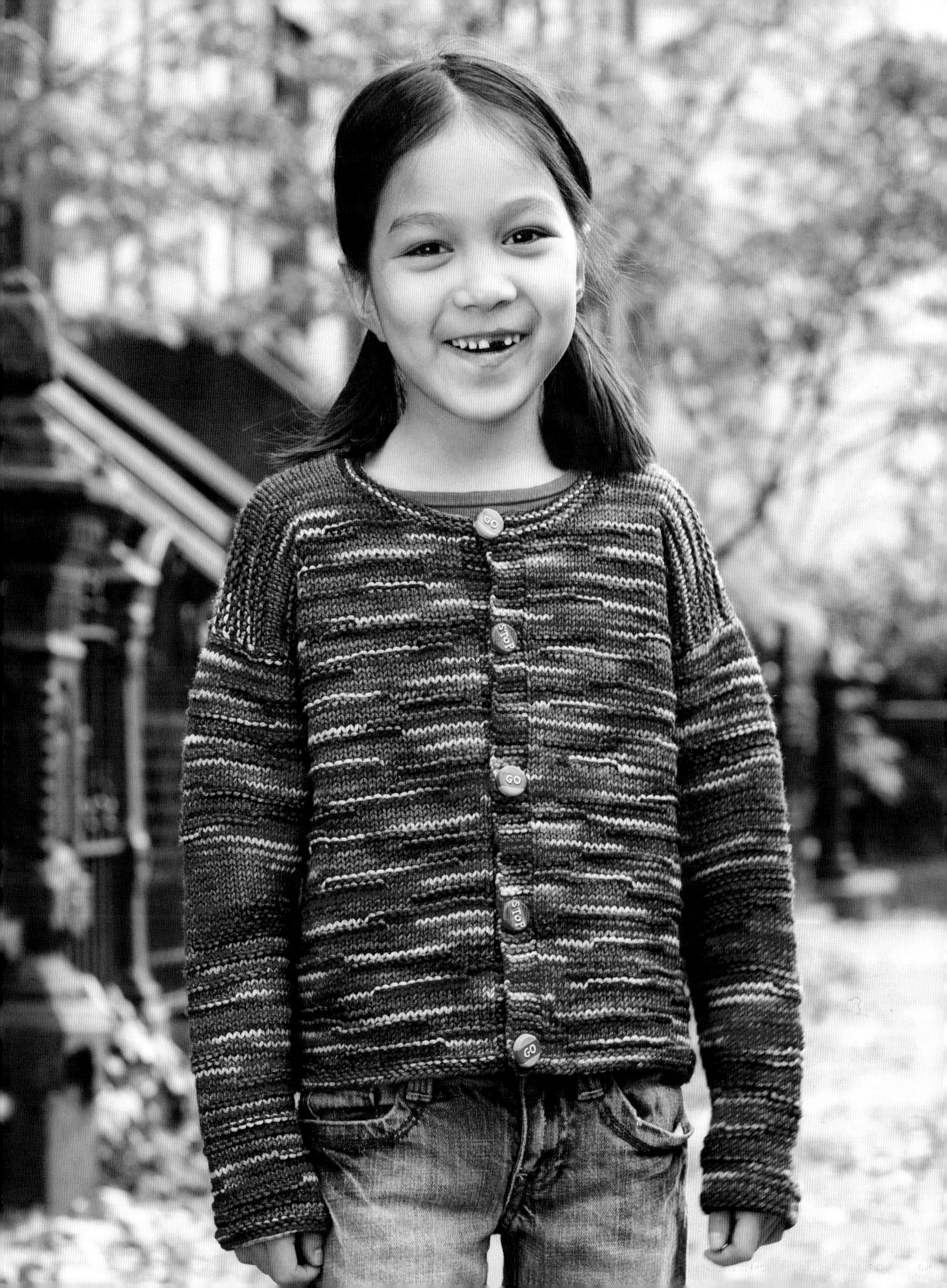
GO
STOP
GO
STOP
GO

BACK

Cast on 70 (75, 80, 85) stitches. Knit three rows (two ridges on right side). Begin stitch pattern as described above. Work even until back measures 8½ (10½, 12, 13)" from cast-on edge. Place marker at each edge for sleeve placement. Continue even until back measures 6½ (7, 7½, 8)" above markers. Place all stitches on holder for shoulders and back neck.

RIGHT FRONT

Cast on 40 (43, 45, 48) stitches. Knit three rows (two ridges on right side). Begin stitch pattern as described above, keeping 5 stitches at center front edge in garter stitch (knit every row). Work even until front measures 8½ (10½, 12, 13)" from cast-on edge. Place marker at armhole edge for sleeve placement. Continue until front measures 4½ (5, 5½, 6)" above marker, ending with a wrong-side row.

Shape Neck

At neck edge, knit across 8 (9, 9, 10) stitches, place these stitches on holder, work in pattern to end. Bind off two

stitches at neck edge four more times—24 (26, 28, 30) stitches remain. Work even until front measures same as back to shoulders. Place all stitches on holder for shoulders. Mark placement for buttons, with the first ½" from lower edge, the top to be in the neckband, and three more evenly spaced between.

LEFT FRONT

Cast on 40 (43, 45, 48) stitches. Knit three rows (two ridges on right side). Begin stitch pattern as described above, keeping 5 stitches at center front edge in garter stitch (knit every row), and working buttonholes over last 5 stitches to correspond to markers on right front, as follows:

Buttonhole Row 1 (RS): Work in pattern to last five stitches, k2tog, yo twice, ssk, k1.

Buttonhole Row 2: K2, (k1, p1) into double yo, k1, work in pattern to end.

Work even until front measures 8½ (10½, 12, 13)" from the cast-on edge. Place marker at armhole edge for sleeve placement. Continue until front measures 4½ (5, 5½, 6)" above marker, ending with a right-side row.

Shape Neck

At neck edge, knit across 8 (9, 9, 10) stitches and place on holder, then bind off two stitches at neck edge four more times—24 (26, 28, 30) stitches remain. Work even until front measures same as back to shoulders. Place all stitches on holder for shoulders.

With right sides together, join fronts to back at shoulders using three-needle bind off (page 31).

SLEEVES

Pick up and knit 65 (70, 75, 80) stitches between sleeve placement markers. Work in pattern while decreasing one stitch each side every sixth row 16 (17, 19, 20) times—33 (36, 37, 40) stitches remain. When sleeve measures 13 (14, 15, 16)" from shoulder or desired length, knit three rows. Bind off. Sew sleeve seams.

NECK EDGING

Pick up and knit 21 (22, 22, 23) stitches along right front neckline, knit across 22 (23, 24, 25) back neck stitches, pick up and knit 21 (22, 22, 23) stitches along left front neckline—64 (67, 68, 71) stitches total. Knit one row. Work buttonhole at right front edge and knit remaining stitches. Knit three rows. Bind off.

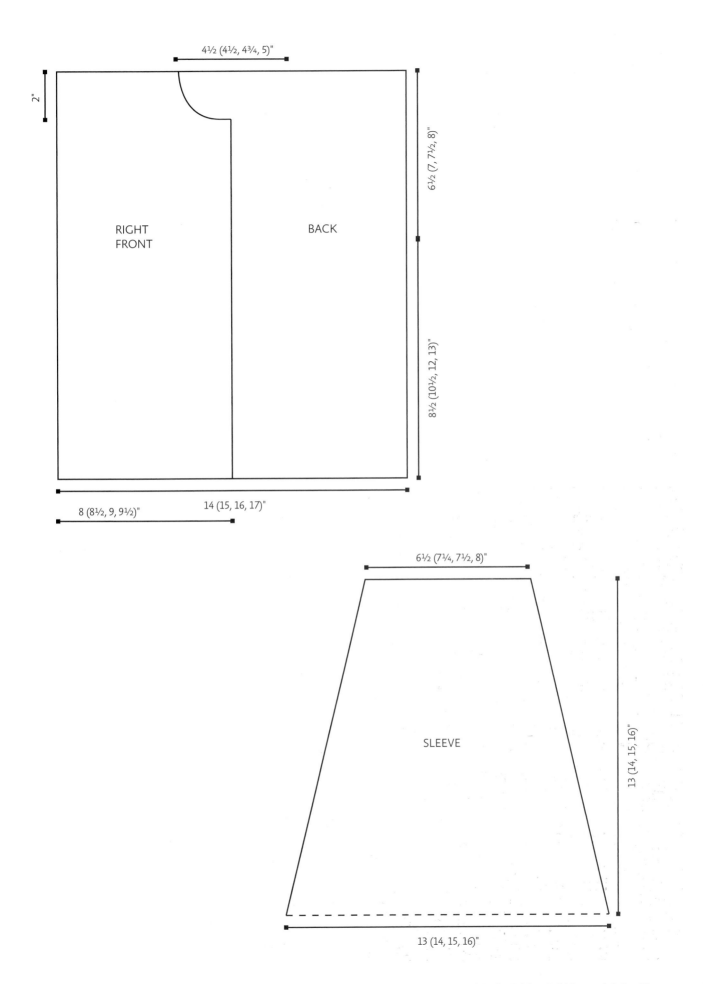

4½ (4½, 4¾, 5)"

2"

RIGHT
FRONT

BACK

6½ (7, 7½, 8)"

8½ (10½, 12, 13)"

8 (8½, 9, 9½)"

14 (15, 16, 17)"

6½ (7¼, 7½, 8)"

SLEEVE

13 (14, 15, 16)"

13 (14, 15, 16)"

chapter

four

KNIT A FEW, SKIP A FEW

Mixing It Up with Slipped Stitches

One of the best things about slipped stitches is how easy they are to work, yet how amazing the results are. A slipped stitch is simply a stitch that is not worked on a particular row or rows, but worked eventually. By the time it is knit or purled, it has been elongated and stretched over one or more rows; it is now in a different row than its neighboring stitches and not likely to be part of any color pooling behind it. When worked in variegated yarns the colors are jumbled, making a blended mix.

Slipped-Stitch Patterns

Unless instructed otherwise, a stitch is slipped from left to right, as if to purl. This moves the stitch without twisting it. When the slipped stitches are worked in a column on top of each other or for several rows, the fabric becomes very compact. If you are using a slipped-stitch pattern for a garment, the shaping may need to be adjusted because a slipped-stitch pattern has more rows per inch. Some stitch patterns instruct you to work extra wraps to prevent this bunching of rows and to allow the slipped stitch to stretch out and lie flat on top of the background. The stitch patterns shown here work well for jackets, cardigans, and blankets. They tend to be more dense than standard knitting, so the compact fabric can become stiff if knit too tightly or on too small needles.

Pleasing Plaid Stitch (multiple of 3)

This stitch pattern is easy to work and can be used in many projects because of the small stitch repeat. Another variation, not shown here, is to work Rows 1 and 2 in a solid and Rows 3 and 4 in variegated. The change in appearance is dramatic.

Row 1 and 3 (RS): K1, *sl 1 as if to purl wyib, k2; repeat from * to last two stitches, sl 1 as if to purl wyib, k1.

Row 2: P1, *sl 1 as if to purl wyif, p2; repeat from * to last two stitches, sl 1 as if to purl wyif, p1.

Row 4: P1, knit to last stitch, p1.

Repeat Rows 1–4 for pattern.

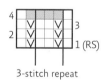

3-stitch repeat

☐ k on RS, p on WS

▨ p on RS, k on WS

☑ sl 1 as if to purl with yarn on WS

Slipped Rib Stitch (multiple of 6 + 4)

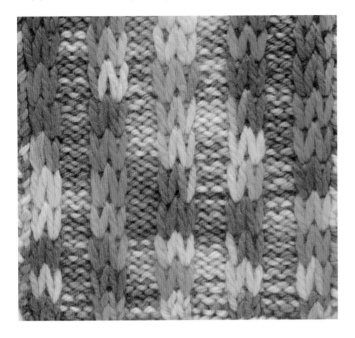

Extra wraps are worked on Row 1 in order to elongate the stitches, which will be slipped over several rows. This prevents the fabric from bunching up and puckering.

Setup row (WS): K4, *p2, k4; repeat from * across.

Row 1 (RS): P4, *k2 wrapping yarn twice around needle, p4; repeat from * across.

Row 2: K4, *sl 2 wyif dropping extra wrap, k4; repeat from * across.

Row 3: P4, *sl 2 wyib, p4; repeat from * across.

Row 4: K4, *sl 2 wyif, k4; repeat from * across.

Repeat Rows 1–4 for pattern.

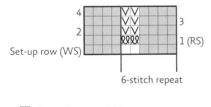

☐ k on RS, p on WS

☐ p on RS, k on WS

☑ sl 1 as if to purl with yarn on WS

▩ k on RS, wrapping yarn twice around needle

Slipped-Woven Stitch (multiple of 4)

This stitch pattern looks almost woven when knit. The stitches are not only slipped, but also passed over other stitches, which rearranges the yarn on the needles and mixes the colors even more.

Setup row (WS): Purl.

Row 1 (RS): *Sl 1, k1, yo, psso, k1 and yo; repeat from * across.

Rows 2 and 4: Purl.

Row 3: K1, *sl 1, k1, yo, psso; repeat from * to last stitch, end k1.

Repeat Rows 1–4 for pattern.

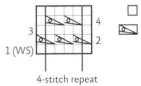

☐ k on RS, p on WS

▨ sl 1 as if to purl, k1, yo, psso, k1 and yo

Garter Slip Stitch (multiple of 8)

Big Bamboo Stitch (multiple of 4 + 2)

This pattern lies flat because it is primarily garter stitch. The slipped stitches add some variety to the front side. With a little effort, the stitch pattern could be worked to make this reversible for blankets, scarves, dishcloths, and place mats.

Row 1 (RS): *K4, k1 wrapping yarn twice around needle, k3; repeat from * across.

Rows 2 and 4: *K3, slip 1 wyif, dropping extra wrap, k4; repeat from * across.

Row 3: *K4, slip 1 wyib, k3; repeat from * across.

Row 4: *K3, slip 1 wyif, k4; repeat from * across.

Row 5: *K1 wrapping yarn twice around needle, k7; repeat from * across.

Row 6: *K7, slip 1 wyif, dropping extra wrap; repeat from * across.

Row 7: *Sl 1 wyib, k7; repeat from * across.

Row 8: Same as Row 6.

Repeat Rows 1–8 for pattern.

The stitches are elongated to allow plenty of length because the stitch is passed over several others. The fabric will have a soft drape, and makes a great throw, shawl, or baby blanket.

Row 1 (WS): Purl.

Row 2: Knit.

Row 3: P1, *p3, p1 wrapping yarn twice around needle; repeat from * to last stitch, p1.

Row 4: K1, *yo, dropping extra loop, sl 1, k3, psso; repeat from * to last stitch, k1.

Repeat Rows 1–4 for pattern.

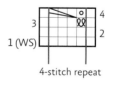

4-stitch repeat

☐   k on RS, p on WS

▦   p on RS, k on WS

▩   p on WS, wrapping yarn twice around needle

⊡   yo

▱   dropping extra loop, sl 1, k3, psso

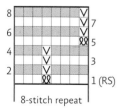

8-stitch repeat

☐   k on RS, p on WS

▦   p on RS, k on WS

☑   sl 1 as of to purl with yarn on WS

▩   k on RS, wrapping yarn twice around needle

Checkered Slip Stitch (multiple of 4 + 3)

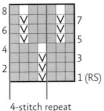

4-stitch repeat

☐ k on RS, p on WS

▨ p on RS, k on WS

☑ sl 1 as if to purl with yarn on WS

These slipped stitches show up well on the reverse stockinette background. They almost look like little hearts lying on the surface.

Rows 1 and 3 (RS): P3, *sl 1 wyib, p3; repeat from * across.

Row 2: K3, *sl 1 wyif, k3; repeat from * across.

Row 4: K3, *p1, k3; repeat from * across.

Rows 5 and 7: P1, *sl 1 wyib, p3; repeat from * to last two stitches, sl 1 wyib, p1.

Row 6: K1, *sl 1 wyif, k3; repeat from * to last two stitches, sl 1 wyif, k1.

Row 8: K1, *p1, k3; repeat from * to last two stitches, p1, k1.

Repeat Rows 1–8 for pattern.

DESERT CAMOUFLAGE VEST

The body of this vest is knit back and forth in one piece, then divided for the armholes, which means there are no seams to interrupt the stitch pattern and less time is spent on finishing. A thorough blocking will remedy the slight tendency of this stitch pattern to skew.

SKILL LEVEL
Experienced

SIZES
Men's Small (Medium, Large, Extra Large, Extra-Extra Large) *Instructions are for smallest size, with changes for other sizes noted in parentheses as necessary.*

FINISHED MEASUREMENTS
Chest: 44½ (48, 52, 56, 60)"
Length (total body): 27 (28, 29, 30, 31)"

MATERIALS
- Lorna's Laces Green Line Worsted 4 MEDIUM (100% organic merino wool; 4 oz/113g, 210 yd/192m): 6 (6, 7, 8, 9) skeins in Roadside Gerry
- Size 7 (4.5mm) 29" circular needle
- Size 7 (4.5mm) 16" circular needle
- Separating zipper to match yarn colors: 25 (26, 27, 28, 29)" long or cut at top edge to correct length
- Tapestry needle
- Sewing needle and thread to match yarn

GAUGE
21 stitches and 28 rows = 4" in Slipped Woven Stitch Pattern

STITCH PATTERN
See Slipped Woven Stitch Pattern on page 53.

NOTES
Body is knit in one piece up to the underarms, then divided for the upper body.

BODY

With 29" circular needle, cast on 234 (254, 274, 294, 314) stitches. Do not join. Working back and forth, knit three rows (two ridges on right side). Beginning with Row 1 of slipped woven stitch and keeping first and last stitches in stockinette stitch, work even until body measures 17 (17½, 18, 18½, 19)" from beginning, ending with a wrong-side row.

Divide for armholes (RS): Work in pattern across 50 (54, 59, 63, 67) stitches for right front, place these stitches on holder, bind off next 16 (18, 18, 20, 22) stitches for underarm, continue across next 102 (110, 120, 128, 136) stitches for back, leave remaining stitches on holder for underarm and left front.

BACK

Working on 102 (110, 120, 128, 136) back stitches only, purl one wrong-side row.

Next row, decrease (RS): K1, ssk, work in pattern to last three stitches, k2tog, k1. Keeping first and last stitches in stockinette stitch, continue to decrease one stitch each side every right-side row 7 (7, 8, 8, 9) times more—86 (94, 102, 110, 116) stitches remain. Work even until upper back measures 10 (10½, 11, 11½, 12)" from underarm bind-off. Place all back stitches on holder.

LEFT FRONT

With right side facing, join yarn at left underarm. Bind off 16 (18, 18, 20, 22) stitches for underarm, continue across remaining 50 (54, 59, 63, 67) stitches. Working on left front stitches only, purl one wrong-side row.

Next row, decrease (RS): K1, ssk, work in pattern to end. Keeping first and last stitches in stockinette stitch, continue to decrease one stitch at armhole edge every right-side row 7 (7, 8, 8, 9) times more—42 (46, 50, 54, 57) stitches remain. Work even until upper front measures 8 (8½, 9, 9½, 10)" from underarm bind-off, ending with a right-side row.

Shape neck (WS): Bind off 10 (11, 12, 13, 13) stitches, work to end. Keeping one stitch at neck edge in stockinette stitch, bind off two stitches at neck edge every wrong-side row 4 (5, 5, 5, 6) times. Work even on remaining 24 (25, 28, 31, 32) stitches until front measures same as back to shoulders. Place all stitches on holder.

RIGHT FRONT

With wrong side facing, join yarn to right armhole, purl to end.

Next row, decrease (RS): Work in pattern to last 3 stitches, k2tog, k1. Keeping first and last stitches in stockinette stitch, continue to decrease one stitch at armhole edge every right-side row 7 (7, 8, 8, 9) times more—42 (46, 50, 54, 57) stitches remain. Work even until upper front measures 8 (8½, 9, 9½, 10)" from underarm bind-off, ending with a wrong-side row.

Shape neck (RS): Bind off 10 (11, 12, 13, 13) stitches, work to end. Keeping one stitch at neck edge in stockinette stitch, bind off two stitches at neck edge every right-side row 4 (5, 5, 5, 6) times. Work even on remaining 24 (25, 28, 31, 32) stitches until front measures same as back to shoulders. Place all stitches on holder.

Join shoulders: With right sides together, join front shoulders to back shoulders with three-needle bind-off (see page 31).

ARMHOLE EDGING

With right side facing and 16" circular needle, pick up and knit approximately 90 (96, 102, 108, 114) stitches around armhole. Place marker and join for working in the round. Purl one round, knit one round, purl one round. Bind off knitwise. Repeat for second armhole.

FRONT EDGINGS

With right side facing and 29" circular needle, pick up and knit approximately 121 (126, 131, 136, 141) stitches along Right Front edge from lower edge to neck. Knit three rows. Bind off. Repeat for Left Front edge, working from neck to lower edge.

NECK EDGING

With right side facing and 16" circular needle, beginning at right front neck, pick up and knit approximately 80 (90, 95, 100, 105) stitches around neck edge. Work in stockinette stitch for 1½", work one row reverse stockinette (turning row), then continue in stockinette stitch for 1½" more. Bind off. Cut yarn, leaving a long tail for seaming.

FINISHING

Block garment flat. Using needle and thread, baste zipper in place so that zipper top extends to collar turning row. Stitch securely along tape edge and next to teeth. Fold collar at turning row over zipper tape to enclose all but the zipper teeth. With a tapestry needle and long tail, whipstitch collar down along inside of neck edge.

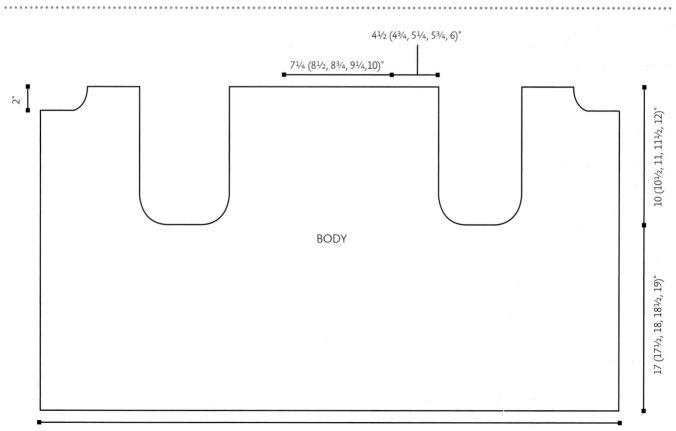

4½ (4¾, 5¼, 5¾, 6)"

7¼ (8½, 8¾, 9¼,10)"

2"

BODY

10 (10½, 11, 11½, 12)"

17 (17½, 18, 18½, 19)"

44½ (48½, 52, 56, 59¾)"

CITY SISTER COIN PURSE

A small, quick project that is as simple as working a rectangle, the coin purse takes on a professional look with the addition of a purse frame.

SKILL LEVEL
Easy

SIZE
One size

FINISHED MEASUREMENTS
5 ½" wide x 5 ½" tall

MATERIALS
- Fiesta Yarns Boomerang (3 LIGHT) (100% extrafine superwash merino wool; 5 oz/142g, 320 yds/2903m): 1 skein in 39142 Jamaican Spice
- Size 6 (4mm) needles
- 1 purse frame (shown: Sunbelt Fastener Company CP06 brass finish)
- Fabric glue
- ½" binder clips, about 8 to 10
- Tapestry needle
- Sewing needle and thread

GAUGE
22 stitches and 40 rows = 4" in Pleasing Plaid Stitch Pattern

STITCH PATTERN
See Pleasing Plaid Stitch Pattern on page 52.

PURSE
Cast on 30 stitches. Work in Pleasing Plaid Stitch pattern until piece measures 11", ending after Row 4. Bind off. Weave in ends.

FINISHING
It is easier to wedge the knit edges into the purse frame before sewing it together. Squeeze fabric glue into the groove of the purse frame. Insert the upper edges of the purse into the groove. Allow it to dry, holding it in place with small binder clips. Protect the frame with a piece of leather or other padding while using pliers to squeeze the groove tightly closed around the purse. Fold in half and sew the side seams below the purse frame.

chapter

five

DIPPING DOWN

Stacking Colors with Tucked-Stitch Patterns

Stitches don't always have to be knit straight across a row. You can knit into the row—or even several rows—below a stitch. Or you can slip stitches, leaving the yarn floats on the right side of the fabric, then catch that float along with a stitch a number of rows later. Or you can knit several times into a stitch to make a decorative pattern. As long as every stitch is used in a way that it won't unravel, stitches can be manipulated in many fun ways.

Fisherman's Rib

Fisherman's Rib is a simple fabric to knit, is reversible, and lies flat. It's a basic knit one, purl one rib except that the knit stitches are worked into the stitch below the one on the needle. This creates a very compact fabric, taking many rows to make an inch, but it is very stretchy, especially widthwise. This fabric will probably not form pools or patterns, but if one begins to form, work from two ends of the yarn and alternate yarns every two rows. (There's nothing wrong with combining techniques!) Fisherman's rib is often used for sweaters, but try it for place mats and blankets, too.

Fisherman's Rib (multiple of 2)

Setup row (do not repeat): Knit.
All rows (reversible): Slip one as if to purl, *p1, k1 in row below stitch; repeat from * across, p1.
Repeat for pattern.

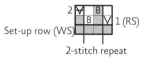

☐ p on RS
☐ p on WS
Ⓑ k1 in row below on RS
Ⓑ k1 in row below on WS
☑ slip 1 purlwise with yarn on WS
☑ slip 1 purlwise with yarn on RS

Leaves and Flowers

When several stitches are worked into one stitch to look like flowers or leaves, the background is usually plain in either stockinette stitch or reverse stockinette stitch. With a variegated background, the colors may form stripes or pools, but this striped background will be broken up by the textured stitches lying on top of it. When multiple stitches are worked into a single stitch, it brings several colors to one spot and adds some bulkiness to the surface, making the flowers or leaves stand out from the background as in the Three-Leaf Stitch (below) and Rosebud Stitch (page 65). When knitting into a stitch that isn't the next one on the needle, be sure to put the right needle directly into the center of the stitch because if it isn't in the middle of the stitch, the stitches below the new stitch could unravel. Insert the needle all the way through the fabric from front to back, rather than trying to catch the stitch in one motion. Making leaves or rosebuds along one panel of a blanket or on the brim of a hat looks nice.

Three-Leaf Stitch (multiple of 18)

Setup Row (WS): Knit.
Row 1: *P4, k1 wrapping yarn three times around needle, p13; repeat from * across.
Row 2: *K13, slip one as if to purl, dropping extra loops off needle, k4; repeat from * across.
Row 3: *P2, insert right-hand needle as if to knit into base of slipped stitch, pull up a long loop onto right-hand needle, p2tog, slip 1 as if to purl wyib, p2tog, insert left-hand needle into base of slipped stitch, pull up a long loop and place on right-hand needle, p11; repeat from * across.

Row 4: *K11, p1, (k1, p1) two times, k2; repeat from * across.

Row 5: *P13, k1 wrapping yarn three times around needle, p4; repeat from * across.

Row 6: *K4, slip 1 as if to purl wyif, dropping extra loops off needle, k13; repeat from * across.

Row 7: *P11, insert right-hand needle into base of slipped stitch, pull up a long loop onto right-hand needle, p2tog, slip 1 as if to purl wyib, p2tog, insert right-hand needle into base of slipped stitch, pull up a long loop onto right-hand needle, p2; repeat from * across.

Row 8: *K2, p1, (k1, p1) two times, k11; repeat from * across.

Repeat Rows 1–8 for pattern.

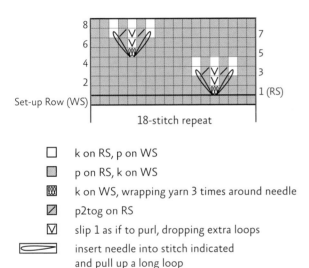

18-stitch repeat

☐   k on RS, p on WS

▨   p on RS, k on WS

▩   k on WS, wrapping yarn 3 times around needle

▨   p2tog on RS

☑   slip 1 as if to purl, dropping extra loops

▱   insert needle into stitch indicated and pull up a long loop

Rosebud Stitch (multiple of 18)

Bobble: (K1, p1, k1, p1, k1) into next stitch, turn; p5, turn; slip 2 tog, k3tog, pass 2 slipped stitches over.

Long Loop: Insert right-hand needle into purl stitch from Row 1 or Row 7, through to back, wrap yarn around needle and pull up loop.

Row 1 (RS): *K13, p1, k4; repeat from * across.

Row 2 and all WS rows: Purl.

Row 3: *K10, slip one, make long loop in next purl stitch from Row 1, move loop and slip stitch to left needle, k2tog, k5, slip one, make long loop in previous purl stitch from Row 1, move loop and slip stitch to left needle, k2tog, k1; repeat from * across.

Row 5: *K13, bobble, k4, repeat from * across.

Row 7: *K4, p1, k13; repeat from * across.

Row 9: *K1, slip one, make long loop in next purl stitch from Row 1, move loop and slip stitch to left needle, k2tog, k5, slip one, make long loop in previous purl stitch from Row 1, move loop and slip stitch to left needle, k2tog, k10; repeat from * across.

Row 11: *K4, bobble, k13; repeat from * across.

Row 12: Purl.

Repeat Rows 1–12 for pattern.

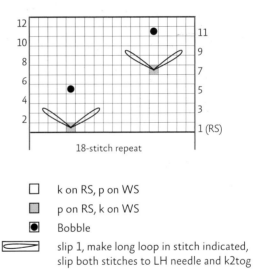

18-stitch repeat

☐   k on RS, p on WS

▨   p on RS, k on WS

⬤   Bobble

▱   slip 1, make long loop in stitch indicated, slip both stitches to LH needle and k2tog

Tucked Stitches

To make a little gather or pucker, you knit into a stitch several rows below and then pull your working stitch snug. This is a fun pattern to work because it looks more complex than it is. It consists of several rows of plain knitting followed by a row where you knit into a stitch many rows below. With so much texture, color pooling is unlikely. This stitch creates an interesting texture for a cuddly baby blanket or a tea cozy.

Tucked-Ridge Stitch (multiple of 6)

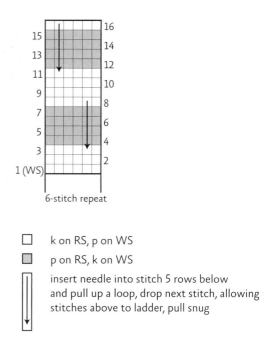

6-stitch repeat

☐ k on RS, p on WS

▦ p on RS, k on WS

⬍ insert needle into stitch 5 rows below and pull up a loop, drop next stitch, allowing stitches above to ladder, pull snug

Rows 1 and 3 (WS): Purl.

Row 2: Knit.

Rows 4 and 6: Purl.

Rows 5 and 7: Knit.

Row 8: *K1, insert needle into stitch five rows below and pull up a loop, drop next stitch, allowing stitches above to ladder, pull snug, k4; repeat from * across.

Rows 9 and 11: Purl.

Row 10: Knit.

Rows 12 and 14: Purl.

Rows 13 and 15: Knit.

Row 16: *K4, insert needle into stitch five rows below and pull up a loop, drop next stitch, allowing stitches above to ladder, pull snug, k1; repeat from * across.
Repeat Rows 1–16 for pattern.

Long Floats

Another method of knitting into a row below is to make long floats on the surface of the fabric. You slip the stitches as if to purl but keep the unworked yarn lying flat across the right side of the fabric. You want to keep this float a little loose, since it will be stretching at a diagonal later. Several rows above the one you are working on, you'll catch the float along with a stitch on the needle. Do not twist the float; it should look as if it is woven behind the newly worked stitch. These floats are at an angle and add very little bulk to the fabric. The Layered Diamond Stitch (page 67, left) has long floats made on wrong-side rows; the Quilted Lattice Stitch (page 67, right) is more delicate and has the look of quilting or embroidery worked on top of a stockinette background. Again, the background may form a little color pooling or stripes, but the surface texture distracts from that and makes the colors all blend together beautifully. Any large knitted piece, such as a sweater or blanket, will show off these patterns well.

Layered Diamond Stitch (multiple of 10)

Rows 1, 3, and 5 (WS): *K1, (p1, k1) two times, sl 5 wyib; repeat from * across.

Rows 2 and 4: *K6, (p1, k1) two times; repeat from * across.

Row 6: *K2, insert needle below three slipped strands and knit these strands together with the next stitch, k3, (p1, k1) two times; repeat from * across.

Rows 7, 9, and 11: *Sl 5 wyib, k1, (p1, k1) two times; repeat from * across.

Rows 8 and 10: *K1, (p1, k1) two times, k5; repeat from * across.

Row 12: *(K1, p1) two times, k3, insert needle below three slipped strands and knit these strands together with the next stitch, k2; repeat from * across.

Repeat Rows 1–12 for pattern.

Quilted-Lattice Stitch (multiple of 6 + 3)

Note: Keep floats loose when slipping stitches on Rows 2 and 6.

Rows 1 and all WS rows: Purl.

Row 2: K2, *slip 5 wyif, k1; repeat from * to last stitch, k1.

Row 4: K4, *insert needle under loose strand and knit it with the next stitch, k5; repeat from * to last five stitches, insert needle under loose strand and knit it with the next stitch, k4.

Row 6: K1, slip 3 wyif, *k1, slip 5 wyif, repeat from * to last five stitches, k1, slip 3 wyif, k1.

Row 8: K1,*insert needle under loose strand and knit it with the next stitch, k5; repeat from * to last two stitches, insert needle under loose strand and knit it with the next stitch, k1.

Repeat Rows 1–8 for pattern.

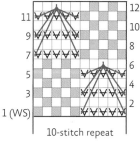

10-stitch repeat

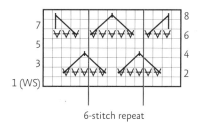

6-stitch repeat

□ k on RS, p on WS

▨ p on RS, k on WS

☒ slip 1 as if to purl with yarn on RS

insert needle under 3 loose strands and knit strands together with stitch

□ k on RS, p on WS

☒ slip 1 as if to purl with yarn on RS

insert needle under loose strand and knit strand together with stitch

AUTUMN HARVEST PLACE MAT

Using cotton yarn makes this place mat practical because it's washable, and the fisherman's rib stitch pattern creates a compact fabric that is reversible and mixes the colors well.

SKILL LEVEL
Intermediate

SIZES
One size

FINISHED MEASUREMENTS
18" wide x 12" tall

MATERIALS
- Schaefer Yarn Laurel 4 MEDIUM (100% mercerized cotton; 8 oz/227g, 400 yds/366m):
- 1 skein (which will make 2 place mats) in Frida Kahlo
- Size 4 (3.5 mm) needles
- Tapestry needle

GAUGE
13 stitches and 32 rows = 4" in Fisherman's Rib Stitch Pattern

STITCH PATTERN
See Fisherman's Rib Stitch Pattern on page 64.

NOTES
The first row is a setup row that is not repeated. Every row thereafter is the same.
K1b = Knit into row below

PLACE MAT
Cast on 64 stitches very loosely. Work in pattern until the piece measures 12" from cast-on. Bind off very loosely in pattern. Weave in ends. Block and lightly starch, if desired.

MONET'S GARDEN QUILTED-LATTICE TOP

This lovely top is worked entirely in the round with no interruption of the stitch pattern and very little finishing needed. The delicate stitch pattern resembles quilting or embroidery on top of a stockinette stitch background.

SKILL LEVEL
Experienced

SIZES
Woman's Extra Small (Small, Medium, Large, Extra Large) *Instructions are for smallest size, with changes for other sizes noted in parentheses as necessary.*

FINISHED MEASUREMENTS
Bust: 31¾ (36, 40¼, 44¾, 49)"

MATERIALS
- Jade Sapphire Silk Cashmere (55% silk, 45% cashmere; 2 oz/55g, 400 yds/366m): 2 (3, 3, 4, 4) skeins in Lagoon #001
- 2 size 3 (3.25mm) circular needles, one 29" and one 16"
- 4 stitch markers, plus one removable stitch marker
- Waste yarn for holder
- Tapestry needle

GAUGE
22 stitches and 32 rows = 4" in Quilted-Lattice Stitch Pattern

QUILTED-LATTICE STITCH PATTERN
(multiple of 6)
Worked in the round; end of round moves every 4 rounds. Keep floats loose when slipping stitches on Rounds 2 and 6.
Rounds 1 and 3: Knit.
Round 2: *Slip 5 wyif, k1; repeat from * around.
Round 4: *K2, insert needle under loose strand and knit it with the next stitch, k3; repeat from * around.
Round 5: Knit to end of round, remove marker, k3. Place marker for beginning of round.
Round 6: *Slip 5 wyif, k1; repeat from * around.
Round 7: Knit.
Round 8: *K2, insert needle under loose strand and knit it with the next stitch, k3; repeat from * around, ending last repeat three stitches before marker; remove marker, place marker to indicate begining of round.
Repeat Rounds 1–8 for pattern.

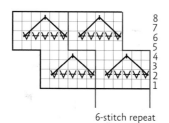

6-stitch repeat

☐   knit

☒   slip 1 as if to purl with yarn on RS

△   insert needle under loose strand and knit strand together with stitch

NOTES

The body is knit on circular needles in one piece to the underarms, the sleeves are worked separately, then all the pieces are joined and worked seamlessly to the neck.

BODY

With a 29" circular needle, cast on 174 (198, 222, 246, 270) stitches. Place marker for beginning of round. Join, being careful not to twist. *Knit one round, purl 1 round; repeat from * twice (three ridges). Change to Quilted Lattice Stitch. Work even until body measures 15 (15 ½, 16, 16 ½, 17)", ending after Round 4 or 8.

Divide Body

Work 81 (93, 105, 117, 129) stitches, bind off 12 stitches for underarm, work to six stitches before marker, bind off 12 stitches for underarm (last six stitches of round and six stitches of next round), removing marker. Set aside.

SLEEVES

With 16" circular needle, cast on 72 (78, 84, 90, 96) stitches. Join, being careful not to twist. Place marker for beginning of round. *Knit one round, purl one round; repeat from * twice (three ridges). Next round: Knit to six

stitches before marker, bind off 12 stitches for underarm (last six stitches of round and six stitches of next round), removing marker. Place remaining 60 (66, 72, 78, 84) stitches on holder and set aside. Make a second sleeve, leaving stitches on needle.

Join for Yoke

With the 29" circular needle and right side facing, continuing with Round 5 or 1 of pattern, work across 75 (87, 99, 111, 123) body stitches to underarm, place marker, work across 60 (66, 72, 78, 84) sleeve stitches from circular needle, place marker, work across 75 (87, 99, 111, 123) body stitches to underarm, work across 60 (66, 72, 78, 84) sleeve stitches from holder, place marker to indicate beg of round—270 (306, 342, 378, 414) stitches.

Continue in Quilted-Lattice Stitch for 3 (3, 3, 2½, 1¾)", ending with an even-numbered round.

If necessary, move the beginning-of-round marker back to original location so that there are an identical number of stitches on the right and left sleeve sections and an identical number of stitches on the front and back sections. At this point, do not move the end-of-round marker at the end of Rounds 5 and 8, but maintain stockinette stitch raglan decreases on either side of markers and established pattern on stitches between raglan decreases.

Decrease Round: *Ssk, work to two stitches before next marker, k2tog, slip marker; repeat from * around—262 (298, 334, 370, 406) stitches. Repeat decrease round every other round 14 (18, 23, 27, 32) more times, changing to 16" circular needles when necessary—150 (154, 150, 154, 150) stitches.

*Knit one round, purl one round; repeat from * twice (three ridges). Bind off loosely. Sew underarm seams. Weave in ends.

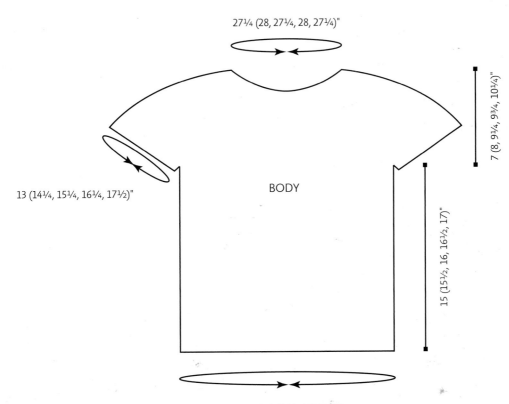

27¼ (28, 27¼, 28, 27¼)"

7 (8, 9¼, 9¾, 10¼)"

13 (14¼, 15¼, 16¼, 17½)"

BODY

15 (15½, 16, 16½, 17)"

31¾ (36, 40¼, 44¾, 49)"

chapter

six

MAKING THE WRONG SIDE RIGHT

Knitting with Float-Stitch Patterns

When you slip a stitch, the working yarn can be held to the front or to the back. If it's held to the wrong side, it doesn't change the appearance of the fabric; the slipped stitches might impact color pooling, but the floats will not show. But when that same float is held to the right side of the work, it adds color that runs in a different direction from the underlying fabric. The float doesn't add much thickness to the fabric because it's just one strand that's not looped or caught or knit in any way. The floats can easily become too tight, though, especially if they're lined up in columns where the same stitches are slipped row after row. Be sure to keep the floats somewhat loose—not so loose that they drape or get caught on things, just loose enough so the fabric lies flat and remains flexible.

Horizontal Floats

Floats can be worked over several stitches. If the background is stockinette, a color pattern may still form, but the horizontal floats on the surface will distract the eye from it.

Checkered Float Stitch (multiple of 8 + 1)

Rows 1, 3, and 5: *K1, slip 3 wyif, k4; repeat from * to last stitch, k1.

Row 2 and all WS rows: Purl.

Rows 7, 9, and 11: *K5, slip 3 wyif; repeat from * to last stitch, k1.

Row 12: Purl.

Repeat Rows 1–12 for pattern.

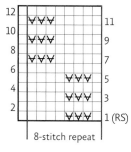

k on RS, p on WS

slip 1 as if to purl with yarn on RS

Single-Stitch Floats

A float may strand over just a single stitch. Here the pattern rows are worked on the wrong side. The effect can be very open and lacy if worked on large needles and would make a pretty scarf, shawl, or lacy throw.

Webbed Float Stitch (multiple of 2 + 2)

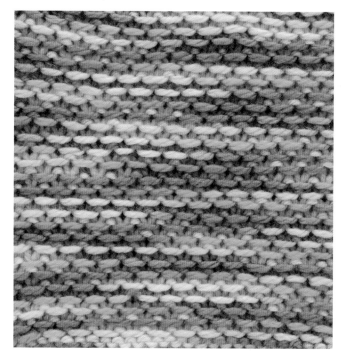

Rows 1 and 3 (RS): Knit.

Row 2: *K1, slip 1 as if to purl wyib; repeat from * to last two stitches, k2.

Row 4: K1, *k1, slip 1 as if to purl wyib, repeat from * to last stitch, k1.

Repeat Rows 1–4 for pattern.

2-stitch repeat

k on RS, p on WS

p on RS, k on WS

slip 1 as if to purl with yarn on RS

Tapestry-Look Floats

If the floats are made on every row, the fabric becomes quite dense and woven-looking. In fact, the knit resembles a tapestry fabric. This pattern is very stable and suitable for coats, purses, tote bags, pillows, and any kind of project where firmness is a plus.

Tapestry Stitch (multiple of 6 + 2)

Row 1 (RS): K1, *k3, slip 3 as if to purl wyif; repeat from * to last stitch, k1.

Row 2: P1, *p1, slip 3 as if to purl wyib, p2; repeat from * to last stitch, p1.

Row 3: K1, *k1, slip 3 as if to purl wyif, k2; repeat from * to last stitch, k1.

Row 4: P1, *p3, slip 3 as if to purl wyib; repeat from * to last stitch, p1.

Row 5: K1, *slip 2 as if to purl wyif, k3, slip one as if to purl wyif; repeat from * to last stitch, k1.

Row 6: P1, *slip 2 as if to purl wyib, k3, slip one as if to purl wyib; repeat from * to last stitch, p1.

Repeat Rows 1–6 for pattern.

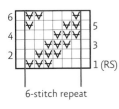

☐ k on RS, p on WS

☑ slip 1 as if to purl with yarn on RS

6-stitch repeat

Floats and Purls

By simply making a purl stitch between the floats, the horizontal lines are accentuated. When the floats line up as they do in this swatch, the fabric becomes less flexible. Sweaters, blankets, pillows, and purses would all show off this pattern beautifully.

Horizontal-Stripe Float Stitch (multiple of 4 + 1)

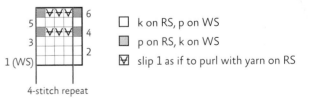

Row 1 and all WS rows: Purl.

Row 2: Knit.

Rows 4 and 6: P1 *slip 3 as if to purl wyif, p1; repeat from * across.

Repeat Rows 1–6 for pattern.

☐ k on RS, p on WS

☐ p on RS, k on WS

☑ slip 1 as if to purl with yarn on RS

4-stitch repeat

Staggered Floats

Staggering the floats allows the fabric to remain stretchy. The floats move gradually in one direction and the colors all shift and mix without pooling. This would be great stitch pattern for a jacket or a warm cardigan.

Stairstep-Float Stitch (multiple of 4 + 2)

Row 1 (RS): K1, *k1, slip 2 wyif, k1; repeat from * to last stitch, k1.

Row 2 and all WS rows: Purl.

Row 3: K1, *k2, slip 2 wyif; repeat from * to last stitch, k1.

Row 5: K1, *slip one wyif, k2, slip one wyif; repeat from * to last stitch, k1.

Row 7: K1, *slip 2 wyif, k2; repeat from * to last stitch, k1.

Row 8: Purl.

Repeat Rows 1–8 for pattern.

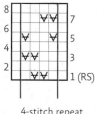

4-stitch repeat

☐ k on RS, p on WS

☑ slip 1 as if to purl with yarn on RS

Floats as Dots

The float in this pattern may appear to be over only one stitch, but it actually is floated all the way across a row, and then back across the next row. The stitches are not knit at all on the float rows, but simply woven to the front then to the back between the stitches. This pattern looks great in hand-dyed yarns. As the background colors form one pattern, the floated yarn on the surface begins forming its own pattern, and the two patterns mix and blend all the colors. With this stitch pattern, be sure to keep the woven rows loose and flexible. Use this stitch for blankets and kids' jackets.

Woven Dot Stitch (even number of stitches)

Row 1 (RS): Knit.

Row 2: Purl.

Row 3: *Slip 1 as if to purl wyib, slip 1 as if to purl wyif; repeat from * across.

Row 4: *Slip 1 as if to purl wyif, slip 1 as if to purl wyib; repeat from * across.

Repeat Rows 1–4 for pattern.

2-stitch repeat

☐ k on RS, p on WS

☑ sl 1 as if to purl with yarn on WS

☑ sl 1 as if to purl with yarn on RS

BERRY FLOAT NECK COZY

The scarf is worked on larger needles than would normally be used for this yarn to give an open and lacy look to the stitches. Be sure to keep the floats loose as you work so that the fabric remains stretchy.

SKILL LEVEL
Easy

SIZES
One Size

FINISHED MEASUREMENTS
4½" wide x 25" long

MATERIALS
- Hand Painted Knitting Yarns Glitter  (50% fine merino wool, 45% nylon, 5% lurex; 3½ oz/100g, 290 yds/265m): 1 skein in Fidelio
- Size 9 (5.5mm) needles
- Two 1" buttons (shown here: JHB Tudor Splendor #33100)
- Tapestry needle

GAUGE
13 stitches and 36 rows = 4" in Webbed Float Stitch Pattern

STITCH PATTERN
See Webbed Float Stitch Pattern on page 76.

NOTES

The scarf is knit lengthwise. To close it, the buttons are pushed through open spaces in the knitting rather than making buttonholes.

Slip 1 wyib = slip one as if to purl with yarn in back

NECK COZY

Cast on 80 stitches. Work in Webbed Float Stitch Pattern for 4½". Bind off. Weave in ends. Block to shape.

FINISHING

Sew two buttons about 1" and 3" from one short end, about 1" from long edge. To wear the scarf, overlap the ends and push the buttons through an open space in the knitting. Or you can overlap the scarf for the desired style, sew it closed, and then sew the buttons through both layers permanently.

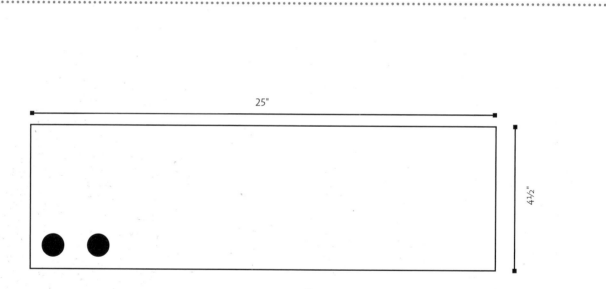

BLUE RAY SOCKS

Variegated yarns tend to make swirling patterns around the circumference of socks. Often the same two or three colors stack on top of each other so that the colors don't look anything like they do in the skein. This stitch pattern helps blend all the colors and make them a little more even.

SKILL LEVEL
Intermediate

SIZES
Women's Medium

FINISHED MEASUREMENTS
7" tall leg, 9" long foot, 8" foot circumference

MATERIALS
- Hand Painted Knitting Yarns Merino Superwash Donegal Tweed Sock Yarn 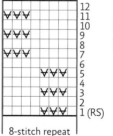 (65% superwash merino wool, 25% nylon, 10% Donegal flecks; 3 ½ oz/100g, 463 yds/423m): 1 skein in Don Giovanni
- Set of four size 1 (2.25mm) double-pointed knitting needles
- Set of four size 3 (3.25mm) double-pointed knitting needles
- Tapestry needle

GAUGE
32 stitches and 48 rounds = 4" in Checkered Float Stitch Pattern

CHECKERED FLOAT STITCH (multiple of 8)
Rounds 1, 3, and 5: *K1, slip 3 as if to purl wyif, k4; repeat from * around.
Round 2 and all even rounds: Knit.
Rounds 7, 9, and 11: *K5, slip 3 as if to purl wyif; repeat from * around.
Round 12: Knit.
Repeat Rounds 1–12 for pattern.

☐ k on RS

☑ slip 1 as if to purl wyif

8-stitch repeat

NOTES
When slipping stitches, carry the yarn on the right side loosely. Slip stitches as if to purl.

RIBBING

Using larger needles, cast on 64 stitches. Divide the stitches evenly on three needles. Join, being careful not to twist stitches. Place marker for beginning of round.

Rounds 1–10: *K2, p2; repeat from * around.

LEG

Change to Checkered Float Stitch Pattern and work until sock measures 8" or desired length.

HEEL

Change to smaller needles. Knit 17 stitches; this is Needle 1. Knit the next 16 stitches; this is Needle 2. Knit remaining 31 stitches onto Needle 3 and increase one stitch at end of row. Now you have a total of 65 stitches. The heel flap will be knitted on Needle 3.

Turn work. Slip 1, and purl back 31 stitches.

HEEL FLAP

Row 1: * Slip 1, k1; repeat from * across.

Row 2: Slip 1, purl across.

Repeat Rows 1 and 2 until heel flap is 2½" tall, or about 30 rows.

Turn heel

Row 1: Slip 1 as if to purl, k19, ssk, k1, turn.

Row 2: Slip 1 as if to purl, p9, p2tog, p1, turn.

Row 3: Slip 1 as if to purl, k10, ssk, k1, turn.

Row 4: Slip 1 as if to purl, p11, p2tog, p1, turn.

Continue in pattern until all stitches have been worked, ending after a purl row.

Knit across to end of needle—20 stitches remain on heel.

GUSSET

With same needle, pick up and knit 15 stitches from side edge of heel flap; this is Needle 1.

With Needle 2, knit across 33 instep stitches.

With Needle 3, pick up and knit 15 stitches from side edge of heel flap, knit across 10 stitches of heel—25 stitches.

Needle 1 also now has 25 stitches.

Place first and last stitches from Needle 2 onto adjacent needles.

Round 1: Needle 1: Knit to last two stitches, k2tog; Needle 2: work in pattern; Needle 3: ssk, knit to end.

Round 2: Knit Needle 1, work Needle 2 in pattern, knit Needle 3.

Repeat Rounds 1 and 2 until 64 stitches remain.

Work even on 64 stitches, working in pattern on Needle 2 and keeping Needles 1 and 3 in stockinette stitch. When foot measures 7" long or 2" shorter than desired length, begin toe shaping.

Round Toe

This toe requires no grafting.

Round 1: *K6, k2tog; repeat from * around—56 stitches. Work two rounds even.

Round 4: *K5, k2tog, repeat from * around—48 stitches. Work two rounds even.

Round 7: *K4, k2tog, repeat from * around—40 stitches. Work two rounds even.

Round 10: *K3, k2tog, repeat from * around—32 stitches. Work two rounds even.

Round 13: *K2, k2tog, repeat from * around—24 stitches. Work two rounds even.

Round 16: *K1, k2tog, repeat from * around—16 stitches. Work two rounds even.

Round 19: K2tog around—8 stitches.

Cut yarn 12" long. Thread through a tapestry needle and pull through remaining stitches twice. Tighten and fasten off. Weave in ends.

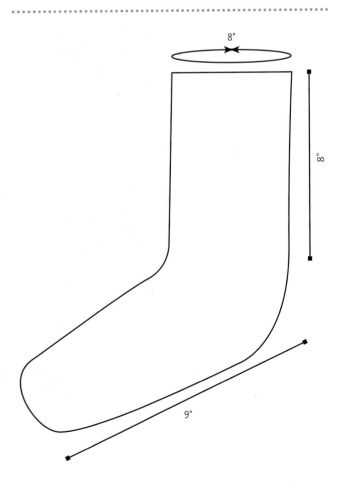

chapter

seven

MANIPULATING COLORS

Customizing with Solids

Most companies that produce hand-dyed yarn offer solid colors to coordinate with their variegated colorways. These hand-dyed solids are actually not true solids, at least not when compared to commercially dyed yarns; they have light and dark tones of one color. Because of these variations, they coordinate beautifully with their variegated counterparts. Commercially dyed solids that really are solid can also be used with variegates, but they tend to be more obvious. Adding a matching solid to your variegated yarn allows you to manipulate the color and prevent pooling at the same time—and customize the colorway to your taste. You can choose one of the dominant or bright colors in the yarn, or choose a color that occurs only every few feet but is your favorite. You can use more than one solid, use a solid as often or as infrequently as you like, or even add a row of it randomly. You have the power to guide the colors to be exactly what you want.

Basket Weave and Solid

In this basket-weave swatch, the solid olive green stripes—almost impossible to see unless you know they are there—are in the "valleys" between the hand-dyed squares. Although not easy to see, the solid yarn has a major impact on the overall color of the knitting, and using a different solid color would change the effect completely. You can use this design for hats, sweaters, and blankets.

Basket-Weave Stitch (multiple of 6)

MC: Variegated
CC: Solid
Rows 1 and 7 (RS): With CC, knit.
Rows 2 and 8: With CC, purl.
Rows 3 and 5: With MC, *k2, p4; repeat from *.
Rows 4 and 6: With MC, *k4, p2; repeat from *.
Rows 9 and 11: With MC, *p3, k2, p1; repeat from *.
Rows 10 and 12: With MC, *k1, p2, k3; repeat from *.
Repeat Rows 1–12 for pattern.

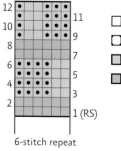
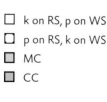

□ k on RS, p on WS
□ p on RS, k on WS
▨ MC
▪ CC

6-stitch repeat

Seed-Stitch Patterns

The Seed Checkers Stitch (below) has a four-row, alternating repeat, and you can use that row repeat as a time to change from variegated to solid. You could also add in other solids that match the variegated yarn. On the Seed-Stitch rows (page 89, left) it's hard to see where one color ends and the next color begins if the colors are changed every row. Choose two colors that match the variegated yarn perfectly (here it's dark brown and olive green) and the colors you don't choose are the ones that will twinkle. When you add a solid, it doesn't have to be less prominent. With the Roman Stitch (page 89, right), you can make the solid color the focal point and let the variegated be the accent color. Here the variegated yarn, highlighted in seed stitch, alternates with wide bands of solid stockinette.

Seed Checkers Stitch (multiple of 8)

MC: Variegated
CC: Solid
Rows 1 and 3 (RS): With MC, *k4, p1, k1, p1, k1; repeat from * across.
Rows 2 and 4: With MC, *k1, p1, k1, p5; repeat from * across.
Rows 5 and 7: With CC, *k1, p1, k1, p1, k4; repeat from * across.
Rows 6 and 8: With CC, *p5, k1, p1, k1; repeat from * across.
Repeat Rows 1–8 for pattern.

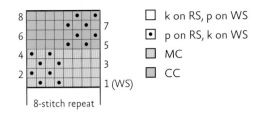

□ k on RS, p on WS
⊡ p on RS, k on WS
▨ MC
▨ CC

8-stitch repeat

Roman Stitch (even number of stitches)

MC: Solid
CC: Variegated
Rows 1 and 3 (RS): With MC, knit.
Rows 2 and 4: With MC, purl.
Row 5: With CC, *k1, p1; repeat from * across.
Row 6: With CC, *p1, k1; repeat from * across.
Repeat Rows 1–6 for pattern.

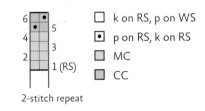

□ k on RS, p on WS
⊡ p on RS, k on RS
▨ MC
▨ CC

2-stitch repeat

Seed Rows (multiple of 2 + 1)

MC: Variegated
A: Solid 1
B: Solid 2
Row 1: With MC, *p1, k1; repeat from * to last stitch, p1.
Row 2: With A, *p1, k1; repeat from * to last stitch, p1.
Row 3: With B, *p1, k1; repeat from * to last stitch, p1.
Row 4: With MC, *p1, k1; repeat from * to last stitch, p1.
Row 5: With A, *p1, k1; repeat from * to last stitch, p1.
Row 6: With B, *p1, k1; repeat from * to last stitch, p1.
Repeat Rows 1–6 for pattern.

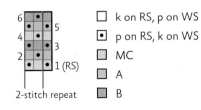

□ k on RS, p on WS
⊡ p on RS, k on WS
▨ MC
▨ A
▨ B

2-stitch repeat

Variegated Lace Stripe

A simple lace pattern can look good in variegated yarn, but adding a solid actually helps give the variegation some continuity. Adding a solid purple to this colorway makes the colors flow throughout the lace rather than stripe or pool. This stitch pattern would be nice for a shawl, a scarf, or an airy cardigan.

Lace-Stripe Stitch (even number of stitches)

MC: Variegated
CC: Solid
Row 1 (RS): With MC, k1, *yo, k2tog; repeat from * to last stitch, k1.
Row 2: With MC, p1, *yo, p2tog; repeat from * to last stitch, p1.
Row 3: With CC, knit.
Row 4: With CC, purl.
Repeat Rows 1–4 for pattern.

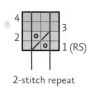

☐ k on RS, p on WS
☑ k2tog on RS, p2tog on WS
⊙ yo
▨ MC
☐ CC

Narrow Stripes

This stitch pattern is simple to work. Using a matching solid lavender for two-row stripes really shows the variegated colors at their best. By choosing which solid to use, it's easy to take charge of the colors in a variegated yarn and make them look the way you want them to. This stitch pattern is versatile and can be used for baby blankets, throws, jackets, and socks.

Narrow-Stripe Stitch (even number of stitches)

MC: Variegated
CC: Solid
Row 1 (WS): With MC, knit.
Rows 2 and 3: With CC, *k1, p1; repeat from * across.
Row 4: With MC, knit.
Repeat Rows 1–4 for pattern.

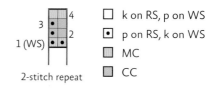

☐ k on RS, p on WS
⊙ p on RS, k on WS
▨ MC
☐ CC

BIG SKY BASKET-WEAVE HAT

The choice for the solid yarn here is one of the shades of blue that is in the variegated yarn. Using the brown that is in the variegated would also be a stunning combination and make the same colorway more masculine.

SKILL LEVEL
Intermediate

SIZE
Average Adult

FINISHED MEASUREMENTS
21" circumference

MATERIALS
- Brown Sheep Lanaloft **4 MEDIUM** (100% wool; 4 oz/113g, 160 yds/146 m): 1 skein each in Twilight LL333 (A) and Big Surf Blue LL48 (B)
- Size 10 (6mm) 16" circular needle
- Set of four size 10 (6mm) double-pointed needles
- Tapestry needle

GAUGE
16 stitches and 20 rounds = 4" in Basket-Weave Stitch Pattern

BASKET-WEAVE STITCH PATTERN

(multiple of 6)

Rounds 1 and 2: With B, knit.

Rounds 3–6: With A, *k2, p4; repeat from * around.

Rounds 7 and 8: With B, knit.

Rounds 9–12: With A, *p3, k2, p1; repeat from * around.

Repeat Rounds 1–12 for pattern.

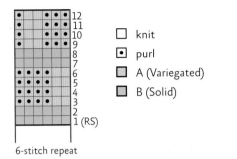

knit

purl

A (Variegated)

B (Solid)

6-stitch repeat

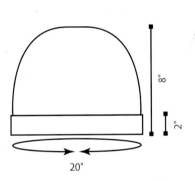

HAT

With B and circular needle, cast on 84 stitches. Place marker to indicate beginning of round. Join, being careful not to twist.

Establish ribbing: *P2, k4; repeat from * around. Work 2" in ribbing. Change to Basket-Weave Stitch and work even for 5", ending after Round 8.

Shape the crown (changing to double-pointed needles when needed):

Round 1: With A, *p3, k2, p2, p2tog, k2, p1; repeat from * around—77 stitches.

Round 2: With A, *p3, k2, p3, k2, p1; repeat from * around.

Round 3: With A, *p1, p2tog, k2, p3, k2, p1; repeat from * around—70 stitches.

Round 4: With A, *p2, k2, p3, k2 p1; repeat from * around.

Rounds 5 and 6: With B, knit.

Round 7: With A, *k1, p1, p2tog, p1, k1, p4; repeat from * around—63 stitches.

Round 8: With A, *k1, p3, k1, p4; repeat from * around.

Round 9: With A, *k1, p3, k1, p1, p2tog, p1; repeat from * around—56 stitches.

Round 10: With A, *k1, p3; repeat from * around.

Rounds 11 and 12: With B, knit.

Round 13: With A, *p2tog, k1, p3, k1, p1; repeat from * around—49 stitches.

Round 14: With A, *p1, k1, p3, k1, p1; repeat from * around.

Round 15: With A, *p1, k1, p1, p2tog, k1, p1; repeat from * around—42 stitches.

Round 16: With A, *p1, k1, p2, k1, p1; repeat from * around.

Rounds 17 and 18: With B, knit.

Round 19: With A, *p2tog, k1; repeat from * around—28 stitches.

Round 20: With A, *p1, k1; repeat from * around.

Round 21: With A, *k2tog; repeat from * around—14 stitches.

Cut yarn, leaving a 10" tail. Using tapestry needle, thread tail through remaining 14 stitches twice. Pull tight and fasten off yarn. Weave in ends.

FIESTA-STRIPED CARDIGAN

The hand-dyed solids in this cardigan have subtle monochromatic variations so they coordinate perfectly with the variegated colorway. By alternating the solids with the variegated evenly, all the colors come together into an interesting pattern. You can choose which solid colors to use to dramatically change the look of the knit fabric.

SKILL LEVEL
Easy

SIZES
Women's Small (Medium, Large, Extra Large, Extra Extra Large) *Instructions are for smallest size, with changes for other sizes noted in parentheses as necessary.*

FINISHED MEASUREMENTS
36 ½ (40, 43 ½, 47 ½, 51)" bust

MATERIALS
- Twisted Sisters Petite Voodoo 3 LIGHT (50% silk, 50% merino wool; 4 oz/113g, 210 yds/192m): 3 skeins in Hand Paint 04 (MC), 2 skeins Indigo (A), 2 skeins Raspberry (B)
- Size 5 (3.75mm) needles
- Size G-6 (4mm) crochet hook
- 4 removable stitch markers or safety pins
- Two 1" buttons
- Tapestry needle

GAUGE
22 stitches and 32 rows = 4" in stockinette stitch

STOCKINETTE-STITCH STRIPES PATTERN
Rows 1, 3, 9, and 11 (right side): With MC, knit.
Rows 2, 4, 10, and 12: With MC, purl.
Rows 5 and 7: With A, knit.
Rows 6 and 8: With A, purl.
Rows 13 and 15: With B, knit.
Rows 14 and 16: With B, purl.

NOTES
The hems of the body and sleeves are meant to roll slightly, or they can be steamed flat if you're using the recommended yarn.

BACK

With MC, cast on 100 (110, 120, 130, 140) stitches. Begin Stockinette-Stitch Stripes, working until back measures 14 (15, 16, 17, 17)" from beginning. Place marker at each edge for armhole placement. Continue to work even until back measures 22 (24, 26, 28, 29)". Place all stitches on holder for shoulders and back neck.

RIGHT FRONT

With MC, cast on 50 (55, 60, 65, 70) stitches. Work same as for back until front measures 19 (21, 23, 25, 26)", ending with a wrong-side row.

Shape neck

At beginning of next right-side row, bind off 10 stitches once, then two stitches every right-side row five times. Work even on remaining 30 (35, 40, 45, 50) stitches until front measures same as back to shoulder. Place stitches on holder for shoulder.

LEFT FRONT

Work same as for Right Front, shaping neck on wrong side rows. Join shoulders using three-needle bind-off (see page 31).

SLEEVES

With MC, pick up and knit 88 (99, 110, 121, 132) stitches between armhole markers. Work in stockinette-stripe pattern while decreasing one stitch at each edge every eight (sixth, fourth, fourth, fourth) row 19 (24, 28, 30, 34) times. Work even on 50 (51, 54, 61, 64) stitches until sleeve measures 20 (20, 19, 18, 17½)" or desired length to cuff. Bind off all stitches. Block garment and sew seams.

FRONT EDGING

With MC and right side facing, pick up and knit 104 (115, 126, 137, 143) stitches along right front edge. Purl one row. Knit one row. Purl one row. Bind off. Repeat for Left Front.

NECK EDGING

With MC and right side facing, pick up and knit approximately 100 stitches around neck edge. Work same as for Front Edging.

Try sweater on to determine button closure placement. Sew one button to Left Front. With crochet hook, slip stitch to attach yarn on right front opposite buttonhole, making a chain long enough to fit around button. Fasten off and secure end of chain to form loop. Weave in ends. Sew button on right front to cover ends of button loop.

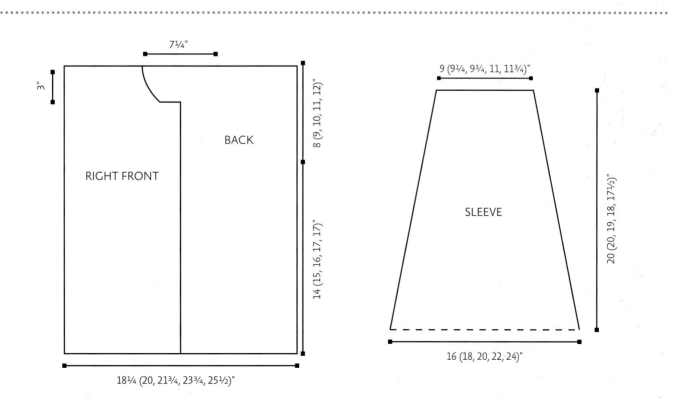

chapter

eight

STRIPE IT UP

Adding Some Zing with Contrasting Solids

When you add a solid color to a variegated yarn, the solid does not have to match one of the colors in the variegated yarn. Sometimes adding a solid that is entirely unrelated to the variegated actually wakes up the colors—it adds something that is unexpected to look at and creates a bit of energy. The options for adding solids are numerous, so feel free to experiment. It doesn't matter what stitch pattern you use; just adding some stripes will make a big impact. The stripes can be as narrow as one row or as wide as several inches.

Linen-Stitch Stripes

The solid rust color added here is not a color in the variegate, though it does blend with its earthy tones. The stitch pattern for the solid yarn, linen-stitch stripes, blends the solid gently into the variegated and back out, helping to make it look right at home. By slipping stitches alternately with the yarn in front, the colors melt into each other, so there is no distinct horizontal line. This easy striped pattern would look nice on sweaters and jackets for the whole family.

Woven-Stitch Pattern (even number of stitches)

MC: Variegated

CC: Solid

Row 1 (RS): With MC, k1, *slip one wyif, k1; repeat from * to last stitch, k1.

Row 2: With MC, p1, *slip one wyib, p1; repeat from * to last stitch, p1.

Rows 3–12: With MC, work in stockinette stitch.

Row 13: With CC, k1, *slip one wyif, k1; repeat from * to last stitch, k1.

Row 14: With CC, p1, *slip one wyib, p1; repeat from * to last stitch, p1.

Row 15: With CC, knit.

Row 16: With CC, purl.

Repeat Rows 1–16 for pattern.

- ☐ k on RS, p on WS
- ☒ slip 1 with yarn on RS
- ☐ MC
- ☐ CC

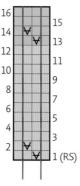

2-stitch repeat

High-Contrast Stripes

This very bold chevron pattern just seems to call out for an equally bold color palette. The chevron's hills and valleys are accentuated by the stripes of the highly contrasting colors. A blanket would look stunning in this pattern.

Chevron Stitch (multiple of 15 + 2)

MC: Variegated

A: Solid 1

B: Solid 2

M1-E (make 1 e-wrap): Make one by wrapping a backwards loop around the right-hand needle.

Rows 1, 3, 5, and 7 (RS): With MC, k1, *k1, m1-E, k5, slip 1 as if to knit, k2tog, psso, k5, m1-E, k1; repeat from * to last stitch, k1.

Rows 2, 4, 6, and 8: With MC, purl across.

Rows 9 and 11: With A, k1, *k1, m1-E, k5, slip 1 as if to knit, k2tog, psso, k5, m1-E, k1; repeat from * to last stitch, k1.

Rows 10 and 12: With A, purl across.

Rows 13 and 15: With B, k1, *k1, m1-E, k5, slip 1 as if to knit, k2tog, psso, k5, m1-E, k1; repeat from * to last stitch, k1.

Rows 14 and 16: With B, purl across.

Repeat Rows 1–16 for pattern.

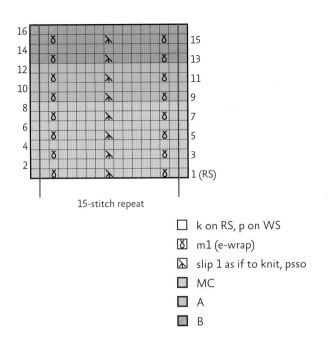

15-stitch repeat

☐ k on RS, p on WS
⊠ m1 (e-wrap)
⊠ slip 1 as if to knit, psso
☐ MC
☐ A
☐ B

Rows 1, 5, and 9 (RS): With MC, k1, *p1, k1; repeat from * to last stitch, k1.

Rows 2, 6, and 10: With MC, p1, *p1, k1; repeat from * across to last stitch, p1.

Rows 3 and 7: With MC, k1, *(k1, p1) three times, k2, (p1, k1) twice; repeat from * to last stitch, k1.

Rows 4 and 8: With MC, p1, *(p1, k1) twice, p2, (k1, p1) 3 times; repeat from * to last stitch, p1.

Rows 11, 15, and 19: With CC, k1, *k1, p1; repeat from * to last stitch, k1.

Rows 12 and 16: With CC, *p1, k1; repeat from * to last two stitches, p2.

Rows 13 and 17: With CC, k1, *(k1, p1) twice, k2, (p1, k1) 3 times; repeat from * to last stitch, k1.

Rows 14 and 18: With CC, p1, *(p1, k1) 3 times, p2, (k1, p1) twice; repeat from * across, p1.

Row 20: Same as Row 16.

Repeat Rows 1–20 for pattern.

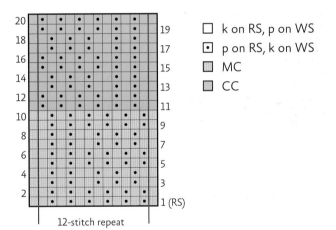

12-stitch repeat

☐ k on RS, p on WS
⊡ p on RS, k on WS
☐ MC
☐ CC

Patterned Stripes

This stitch pattern has two slightly different designs of ten rows each so changing the colors for each design creates a stripe pattern that is bold and clear. Choose a contrasting color that really shows up against the variegated. The strong horizontal stripes work well for children's clothing as well as for blankets, hats, socks, and purses.

Retro Stitch (multiple of 12 + 2)

MC: Variegated
CC: Solid

Herringbone Stripes

All the colors in this variegated yarn are grayed and sub-dued. The choice of a solid green that is much lighter than the green in the variegate helps the colors work together and highlights the herringbone pattern. For this pattern, use a larger needle than recommended for your yarn because the stitch pattern tightens the gauge. Knit firmly, this would be a good pattern for a tote bag or a purse; with a looser gauge, it would work well for a scarf or a blanket.

Herringbone Stitch (any number of stitches)

MC: Variegated
CC: Solid
Rows 1 and 3 (RS): With MC, *k2tog through back loops, leaving second stitch on the left needle; repeat from * to last stitch, k1.
Rows 2 and 4: With MC, *p2tog, leaving second stitch on the left needle; repeat from * to last stitch, p1.
Row 5: With CC, *k2tog through back loops, leaving second stitch on the left needle; repeat from * to last stitch, k1.
Row 6: With CC, *p2tog, leaving second stitch on the left needle; repeat from * to last stitch, p1.
Repeat Rows 1–6 for pattern.

Framing Stripes

One way to make variegated colors stand out is to add a solid color in a dark, rich version of one of the colors in the variegated. Or use white or black, which will make almost any colorway look framed and quite stunning. In the swatch below, the navy offers a strong contrast to the vibrant rainbow colors, and makes them look even brighter. Each stripe of color is just one row. Use this stitch pattern in any pattern that calls for stockinette, simply using two colors instead of one.

Single-Row Stripes (odd number of stitches)

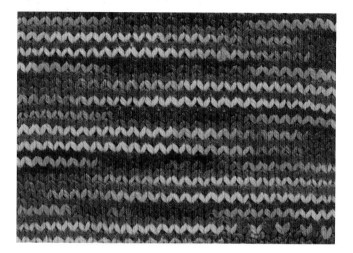

MC: Variegated
CC: Solid
Note: This pattern must be worked on double-pointed or circular needles.
Row 1 (RS): With MC, knit.
Row 2 (RS): Slide stitches to other end of needle. With CC, knit.
Row 3: With MC, purl.
Row 4: Slide stitches to other end of needle. With CC, purl.
Repeat Rows 1–4 for pattern.

☐ MC
☐ CC
⊠ k2tog through back loops, leaving second stitch on need
⊠ p2tog, leaving second stitch on needle

stitch repeat over any number of stitches

NOTE: knit last stitch of each RS row, purl last stitch of each WS row

Lace Stripes

In the striped design below, the solid dark purple is not one of the colors in the variegated yarn, but is related to its many shades of purple and pink so it blends in, rather than contrasts. The stitch pattern changes every six rows so that is also when the colors change. This pattern is not a particularly open lace stitch. It would make a nice blanket, twin set, hat, scarf, or shawl.

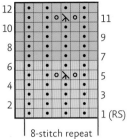

	k on RS, p on WS
•	p on RS, k on WS
o	yo
⋏	slip 1 as if to knit, k2tog, psso
	MC
	CC

8-stitch repeat

Triangle-Lace Stitch (multiple of 8 + 1)

MC: Variegated

CC: Solid

Rows 1 and 3 (RS): With MC, *k1, p1; repeat from * to last stitch, k1.

Rows 2, 4, and 6: With MC, *p1, k1; repeat from * to last stitch, p1.

Row 5: With MC, *k1, p1, yo, slip 1 as if to knit, k2tog, psso, p1, k1, p1; repeat from * to last stitch, k1.

Rows 7 and 9: With CC, *k1, p1; repeat from * to last stitch, k1.

Rows 8 and 10: With CC, *p1, k1; repeat from * to last stitch, p1.

Row 11: With CC, *k1, p1, yo, slip 1 as if to knit, k2tog, psso, p1, k1, p1; repeat from * to last stitch, k1.

Row 12: Same as Row 8.

Repeat Rows 1–12 for pattern.

MARBLEIZED BABY SWEATER

Horizontal stripes aren't always flattering on adults, but they look great on babies. These stripes have a slight blending between the colors, however, which softens the harsh stripe, making it a good choice for adults as well. Choose a solid yarn that is not related to the variegated to make a bold statement, or something in the same color family for a gentle look.

SKILL LEVEL
Intermediate

SIZES
6 months (1 year, 2 years, 3 years) *Instructions are for smallest size, with changes for other sizes noted in parentheses as necessary.*

FINISHED MEASUREMENTS
20 (22, 24, 26)" chest

MATERIALS
- Lorna's Laces Shepherd Bulky  (100% superwash wool; 4 oz/113g, 140 yds/128m): 2 (2, 2, 3) skeins in Purple Club (MC), 1 skein in Douglas Fir (CC)
- Size 9 (5mm) 24" circular needle
- 3 stitch holders
- 4 (5, 5, 6) one-inch buttons
- Tapestry needle

GAUGE
16 stitches and 22 rows = 4" in Woven-Stitch Pattern

STITCH PATTERN
See Woven-Stitch Pattern on page 100.

NOTES
The body is knit back and forth in one piece to the underarms, then divided for armholes and upper body. The sleeves are knit separately and sewn in. Use superwash wool yarn so that the garment and the edges can be steamed to block flat.

BODY
With CC and circular needle, cast on 80 (88, 96, 104) stitches. Do not join. Purl one row (wrong side). Begin woven-stitch pattern. Work even until piece measures 6 (6½, 7, 8)". Work across 20 (22, 24, 26) stitches for right front, place on holder, work across 40 (44, 48, 52) stitches for back, place remaining 20 (22, 24, 26) stitches on holder for left front.

Continue to work even on back stitches until upper back measures 4 (5, 5½, 6)". Place all stitches on holder for shoulders and back neck.

LEFT FRONT
Replace Left Front stitches on needle. Beginning with right side facing, join yarn and work even until left front measures 2 (3, 3½, 4)", ending with a right-side row.

Shape neck (wrong side)
Bind off four stitches at beginning of the next wrong-side row, then two stitches at beginning of the following two-wrong side rows. Work even on remaining 12 (14, 16, 18) stitches until front measures the same as back to shoulders.

RIGHT FRONT
Replace Right Front stitches on needle. Beginning with wrong side facing, join yarn and work as for Left Front, reversing neck shaping.

Join front shoulders to back shoulders using three-needle bind-off (see page 31).

SLEEVE
With CC, cast on 20 (28, 30, 32) stitches. Purl one row (WS). Begin Woven-Stitch Pattern. Increase one stitch at each edge every fourth (fourth, sixth, sixth) row 6 (6, 7, 8) times. Work even on 32 (40, 44, 48) stitches until sleeve measures 6½ (7, 10, 12)". Bind off all stitches. Sew sleeve seam. Sew sleeve into armhole.

COLLAR

With MC and wrong side of neck facing, pick up and knit 12 stitches along front neck edge, knit across 16 stitches along back neck edge, pick up and knit 12 stitches along front neck edge—40 stitches. Work nine rows in stockinette stitch. Change to CC. Work Rows 13 and 14 of Woven-Stitch Pattern. Bind off loosely.

BUTTONHOLE BAND

(Right Front for girls, Left Front for boys)
With MC and right side facing, pick up and knit 32 (38, 42, 48) stitches along front edge. Knit three rows.
Buttonhole row: Knit 2 (2, 2, 3), *yo, k2tog, k7 (6, 7, 6); repeat from * to last 3 (4, 4, 5) stitches, yo, k2tog, knit to end. Knit one row. Bind off.

BUTTONBAND

Pick up stitches same as for Buttonhole Band. Knit five rows. Bind off. Sew buttons to correspond with buttonholes. Weave in ends.

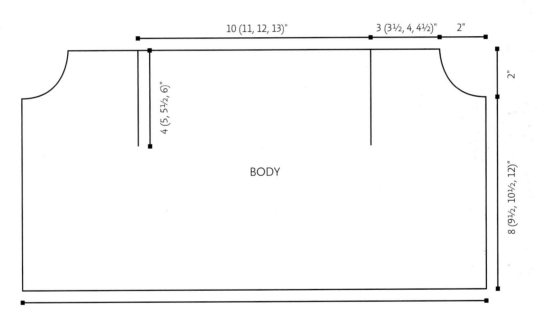

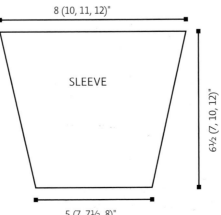

MIGHTY MOUNTAIN CHEVRON THROW

The chevron zigzags in this pattern keep all the variegated colors well mixed. The solid yarns do not match any of the colors in the variegated, but they do complement it well.

SKILL LEVEL
Intermediate

SIZES
One size

FINISHED MEASUREMENTS
43" wide x 58" long

MATERIALS
- Schaefer Yarn Elaine  (99% merino wool, 1% nylon; 8 oz/227g, 300 yds/274m): 3 skeins in Nellie Bly (A), 2 skeins in Indigo (B), 2 skeins in Almond (C)
- Size 10½ (6.5mm) 29" circular knitting needle
- Tapestry needle

GAUGE
14 stitches and 17 rows = 4" in Chevron-Stitch Pattern, blocked

STITCH PATTERN
See Chevron Stitch Pattern on page 100.

NOTES
M1-E (make one e-wrap) = make one by wrapping a backwards loop around the right needle.

THROW
With A and circular needle, cast on 152 stitches. Do not join. Begin Chevron Stitch. Work in pattern for approximately 60", ending after Row 8. Bind off.

chapter

nine

NOT-SO-CLASSIC
FAIR ISLE

Plain and Fancy, Unique and Dramatic

Knitting a Fair Isle design with variegated yarn makes it look special. A simple Fair Isle, usually worked with two colors in stockinette, can now have half a dozen colors, and the design will look as if you chose all those colors, coordinating them perfectly—and also did all the work of knitting them and weaving in all the ends.

For Fair Isle colorwork, charts are the easiest way to read the pattern. Yarns are carried across the back of the work. Keep the yarns loose enough that the fabric does not pucker and the knitting stays stretchy, but not so loose that your stitches become loose and sloppy. If the design requires carrying a color for more than one inch, twist the yarns to catch the unused yarn on the wrong side to avoid long floats. Wool yarns are the most forgiving and easiest to work with in Fair Isle.

High-Contrast Colors

In a Fair Isle design, it's very important to choose a solid color or colors that contrast with the variegated. If the solids are closely related to the variegated, it will be hard to see the Fair Isle design, both while knitting and in the finished project. This is the time to think completely outside the box and choose a color you would least expect: green to go with the pink and lavender variegated (below), dark purple for a bright blue and green mixture (right, top), pale lavender for an intense blue-green-purple-pink yarn (right, bottom), or light green and dark brown to go with a brown and blue yarn (page 113, top). As long as the colors don't match, you'll be able to see the Fair Isle pattern.

Houndstooth Fair Isle (multiple of 8 + 2)

MC: Solid
CC: Variegated

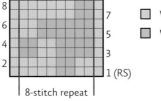

☐ With MC, k on RS, p on WS
☐ With CC, k on RS, p on WS

8-stitch repeat

Circles Fair Isle (multiple of 8 + 1)

MC: Solid
CC: Variegated

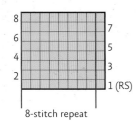

☐ With MC, k on RS, p on WS
☐ With CC, k on RS, p on WS

8-stitch repeat

Triangles Fair Isle (multiple of 6)

MC: Variegated
CC: Solid

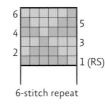

☐ With MC, k on RS, p on WS
☐ With CC, k on RS, p on WS

6-stitch repeat

Checkered Fair Isle (multiple of 8 + 6)

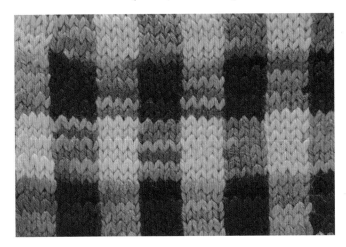

MC: Variegated
A: Solid 1
B: Solid 2

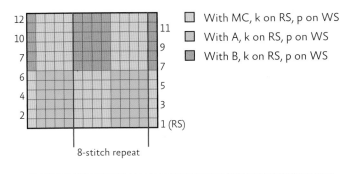

With MC, k on RS, p on WS
With A, k on RS, p on WS
With B, k on RS, p on WS

8-stitch repeat

Candy Dots Fair Isle

A simple Fair Isle pattern that has just one stitch in a different color can be dramatic. When knit with variegated yarn, it looks as if each dot is knit in a different color. In traditional Scandinavian knitting, when the dots are worked in white against a dark background, the pattern is called lice stitch.

Candy Dots Fair Isle (any number of stitches)

MC: Solid
CC: Variegated

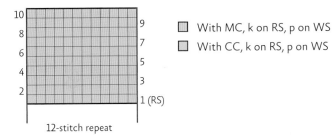

With MC, k on RS, p on WS
With CC, k on RS, p on WS

12-stitch repeat

Chess Fair Isle

For a Fair Isle using two variegates, choose colorways that are completely unrelated. If one yarn has pastels, for example, don't use a yarn that has dark shades of those same colors; instead, try one with completely different colors so that the two variegates have plenty of contrast. In the pattern below, a variegate of bright red, orange, yellow, green, blue, and purple was paired with one in shades of brown. If you find that after a few rows it's difficult to see the Fair Isle design, you need to rethink one of the color choices.

Chess Fair Isle (multiple of 4)

MC: Variegated
CC: Solid

With MC, k on RS, p on WS
With CC, k on RS, p on WS

4-stitch repeat

AMETHYST HOUNDSTOOTH VEST

This vest is made with a traditional sock yarn, but it is not knit as tightly as socks are so it shouldn't take long to knit. The Fair Isle pattern is only used for the front of the vest, the back is knit in solid purple in plain stockinette.

SKILL LEVEL
Intermediate

SIZES
Woman's Small (Medium, Large, Extra Large)
Instructions are for smallest size, with changes for other sizes noted in parentheses as necessary.

FINISHED MEASUREMENTS
36 (40, 44, 48)" chest

MATERIALS
- Brown Sheep Wildfoote (75% washable wool, 25% nylon; 2 oz/50g, 215 yds/197m): 4 (5, 5, 6) skeins SY30 Vinca Minor (MC) and 2 skeins SY900 Lilac Desert (CC)
- Two size 4 (3.5mm) circular needles, one 29" and one 16"
- 9 removable stitch markers or safety pins
- 4 stitch holders
- Nine ½" buttons (shown here: JHB Small Heart Buttons #90890)
- Tapestry needle

GAUGE
24 stitches and 36 rows = 4" in Houndstooth Fair Isle Pattern

STITCH PATTERN
See Houndstooth Fair Isle Pattern on page 112.

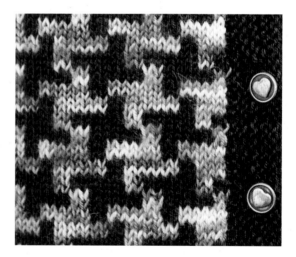

BACK

With 29" circular needle and MC, cast on 111 (129, 144, 159) stitches. Working back and forth, work in garter stitch for 1". Change to stockinette stitch and work even until back measures 14 (14½, 15, 15½)" from beginning, ending with a wrong-side row.

Shape Armholes

Bind off 7 (10, 12, 14) stitches at beginning of next two rows. Decrease one stitch at each edge every right-side row 7 (9, 12, 14) times. Work even on 83 (91, 96, 103) stitches until armhole measures 8 (8½, 9, 9½)". Place 24 (26, 28, 30) stitches on each end on holders for shoulders and center 35 (39, 40, 43) stitches on holder for back neck.

RIGHT FRONT

With 29" circular needle and MC, cast on 50 (58, 66, 74) stitches. Working back and forth, work in garter stitch for 1". Change to Houndstooth Fair Isle Pattern and work even until front measures 14 (14½, 15, 15½)" from beginning, ending with a wrong-side row.

Shape Armhole and V-neck

Decrease armhole same as for back AT THE SAME TIME decrease one stitch at neck edge on fourth row then sixth row alternately until 12 (13, 14, 16) decreases have been worked—24 (26, 28, 30) stitches remain when all shaping is complete. Continue in pattern until armhole measures same as back to shoulders.

LEFT FRONT

Work same as for Right Front, reversing shaping. Join shoulders using the three-needle bind-off (see page 31). Block garment and sew side seams.

BUTTON AND BUTTONHOLE PLACEMENT

Place marker ½" from lower front edge on Right Front. Place marker at first neck decrease. Measure and evenly space seven more markers between these two for a total of nine buttonholes.

FRONT AND NECK EDGINGS

Using 29" circular needle, with right side facing pick up and knit approximately 122 (127, 132, 138) stitches from right front hem to shoulder seam, knit across 35 (39, 40, 43) back neck stitches, pick up and knit approximately 122 (127, 132, 138) stitches from shoulder seam to left front hem—279 (293, 304, 319) stitches. Knit three rows. Buttonhole row: Knit across, working (k2tog, yo) at each marker on right front. Continue to knit every row until edging measures 1". Bind off. Sew buttons on Left Front opposite buttonholes.

ARMHOLE EDGINGS

Using 16" circular needle, pick up and knit approximately 90 (96, 102, 106) stitches around armhole. Join for working in the round. Work in garter stitch (purl one round, knit one round) until edging measures 1". Bind off. Weave in ends.

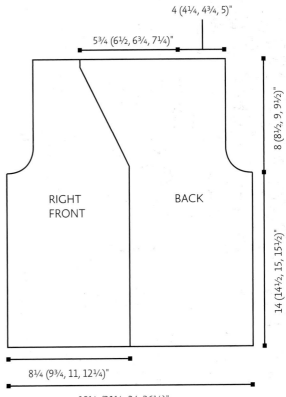

4 (4¼, 4¾, 5)"

5¾ (6½, 6¾, 7¼)"

8 (8½, 9, 9½)"

RIGHT FRONT

BACK

14 (14½, 15, 15½)"

8¼ (9¾, 11, 12¼)"

18½ (21½, 24, 26½)"

CHECKS-AND-BALANCES LAPTOP CASE

Fair Isle knitting is thicker than plain stockinette stitch because the unused yarn is carried across the back of the work. Felting the knitting makes it even thicker. Here, combining these two techniques is advantageous because cushioning is just what you want for a laptop case.

SKILL LEVEL
Experienced

SIZE
One size

FINISHED MEASUREMENTS
14" wide x 12" high

MATERIALS
- Mountain Colors Mountain Goat (4 MEDIUM) (55% mohair, 45% wool; 3 ½ oz/100g, 230 yds/210m): 2 skeins in Mountain Tango (MC), 1 skein in Berry (A), 1 skein in Blue/Green (B)
- One pair size 9 (5.5mm) knitting needles
- One 24" long separating zipper
- Sewing needle and thread
- 2 yards heavy cotton yarn
- Tapestry needle
- Single blade razors `

GAUGE
20 stitches and 28 rows = 4" in Checkered Fair Isle Pattern, before felting

STITCH PATTERN
See Checkered Fair Isle Pattern on page 113.

NOTES
The case is knit as a long rectangle that blocks to 22" wide by 36" long before felting.

CASE
Using MC, cast on 110 stitches. Work in pattern for 36", ending after Row 12. Bind off using MC. Block thoroughly using steam. Fold in half, wrong sides together. Thread the heavy cotton yarn through the tapestry needle. Using 1" long stitches, whipstitch the rectangle closed on three sides. This will prevent the edges from distorting and getting wavy during the felting process.

Using a washing machine, wash in hot water for a regular cycle, removing frequently to check for size. Remove when knitted fabric measures about 15" wide by 23" tall or double the size of your laptop. Rinse and allow to dry. Shave the right side of the rectangle to smooth it.

Remove the cotton yarn. Center the zipper along the top edge of the case and down the sides. Pin the zipper in place all around, then unzip the zipper for easier sewing. Sew the zipper along the edges using a sewing machine or by hand. Zip the case closed. Sew the remaining openings on both sides of the case.

chapter

ten

HOLES ARE BEAUTIFUL

Color in Lace-Stitch Patterns

Lace knitting and hand-dyed yarns can be a beautiful match but not every hand-dyed yarn will look good in every lace pattern. To find a good match, think about lace patterns as being one of two types: repetitive, which are easy to see; and irregular, which are complex or changing. Repetitive patterns have easily distinguishable shapes, such as diamonds, squares, stripes, or chevrons. Their recurring patterns are easy to see even when knit in many colors. An irregular lace pattern is one in which eyelets form either pictures, such as fish or trees, or letters that spell out a name, or one with a very large or complex pattern that requires some intense focus in order to see the design. Active colorways will compete with an irregular lace pattern. The movement of the color and the action of the lace interacting together make it difficult for your eyes to discern either one. The most effective combinations of hand-dyed yarns and lace are calm colorways with any lace pattern and active colorways with repetitive lace patterns. Also think about texture: Consider a yarn with a lot of surface texture, such as mohair or bouclé an active colorway and choose a repetitive lace pattern. Much detail can be lost in lace with fuzzy or novelty yarns. Always knit a swatch to help decide what type of lace works best with your colorway.

Calm Colorway with Irregular Lace

This lace pattern is simple but irregular because it is difficult to see the eyelets even when knit in a calm colorway. This stitch pattern blends the colors well and would make a nice fabric for sweaters, blankets, hats, and socks.

Ribbed Lace (multiple of 4 + 2)

Row 1: *P2, yo, ssk; repeat from * to last two stitches, p2.
Row 2: K2, *p2, k2; repeat from * across.
Row 3: *P2, k2tog, yo; repeat from * to last two stitches, p2.
Row 4: Same as Row 2.
Repeat Rows 1–4 for pattern.

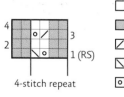

☐	k on RS, p on WS
▨	p on RS, k on WS
☑	k2tog
◺	ssk
⊡	yo

4-stitch repeat

Calm Colorway with Repetitive Lace

This lace pattern would show up well in almost any type of colorway. Knit in a calm colorway, one where the colors vary but all are the same intensity, it would make a nice shawl or feminine sweater.

Starburst Lace (odd number of stitches)

Row 1 (RS): K1, *yo, slip one as if to knit, k1, yo, psso both the knit stitch and the yo; repeat from * across.
Row 2: *P2, drop the yo of previous row; repeat from * to last stitch, p1.
Row 3: K2, *yo, slip one as if to knit, k1, yo, psso both the knit stitch and the yo; repeat from * to last stitch, k1.
Row 4: P3, *drop the yo of previous row, p2; repeat from * across.
Repeat Rows 1–4 for pattern.

☐	k on RS, p on WS
⊡	yo
◩	slip 1 as if to knit, k1, yo, psso both the knit stitch and yo
▼	drop stitch

stitch repeat

Note: Stitch count changes at end of each row; stitches are added on RS rows and dropped on WS rows.

Calm Colorway with Irregular Lace

The stitch pattern has an obvious repeat, but the details would be lost in a more active colorway. Here the colors blend together enough to use the fairly busy lace pattern.

Butterfly Lace (multiple of 8 + 7)

Rows 1 and 3 (RS): K1, *k2tog, yo, k1, yo, ssk, k3; repeat from * across, end k2tog, yo, k1, yo, ssk, k1.
Rows 2 and 4: P3, *slip one wyif, p7; repeat from * to last four stitches, slip one wyif, p3.
Rows 5 and 7: K5, *k2tog, yo, k1, yo, ssk, k3; repeat from * to last two stitches, k2.
Rows 6 and 8: P7, *slip one wyif, p7; repeat from * across.
Repeat Rows 1–8 for pattern.

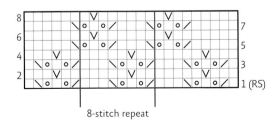

8-stitch repeat

□   k on RS, p on WS
☑   slip 1 as if to purl with yarn on WS
◉   yo
◪   k2tog
◣   ssk

Active Colorways with Repetitive Lace

For active colorways, choose a bold lace pattern, one that is repetitive and easy to see, to make the color the real focal point. For example, an active colorway in shades of turquoise knit in a repetitive lace pattern (below) could be used for blankets or edgings on sweaters. For a colorway with many contrasting colors (page 124, left), a challenging one to knit in lace, choose a very repetitive, easy-to-see pattern so that both the colors and the lace can be appreciated. In a rainbow colorway (page 124, right), the bright colors will fight for attention with a lace pattern, so use the largest lace pattern that your project will allow, not something intricate or detailed. The large Leaning-Squares Stitch Pattern worked in any colorway would make an interesting vest in a lighter-weight yarn or a blanket in heavier yarn.

Little Fan (multiple of 12)

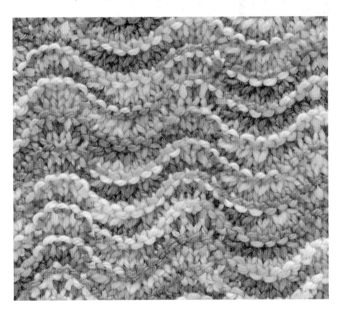

Row 1 (RS): Knit.
Row 2: Purl.
Row 3: *(K2tog) twice, (yo, k1) four times, (k2tog) twice; repeat from * across.
Row 4: Knit.
Repeat Rows 1–4 for pattern.

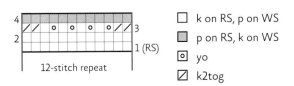

12-stitch repeat

□   k on RS, p on WS
▧   p on RS, k on WS
◉   yo
◪   k2tog

Diaphanous Lace (multiple of 12 + 2)

Row 1 and all WS rows: Purl.

Row 2: K1, *k4, k2tog, yo, k1, yo, ssk, k3; repeat from * to last stitch, k1.

Row 4: K1, *k3, k2tog, k1, yo, k1, yo, k1, ssk, k2; repeat from * to last stitch, k1.

Row 6: K1, *k2, k2tog, k2, yo, k1, yo, k2, ssk, k1; repeat from * to last stitch, k1.

Row 8: K1, *k1, k2tog, k3, yo, k1, yo, k3, ssk; repeat from * to last stitch, k1.

Row 10: K1, k2tog, k4, yo, k1, yo, k4, *slip 1 as if to knit, k2tog, psso, k4, yo, k1, yo, k4; repeat from * to last two stitches, ssk.

Row 12: K1, *k1, yo, ssk, k7, k2tog, yo; repeat from * to last stitch, k1.

Row 14: K1, *k1, yo, k1, ssk, k5, k2tog, k1, yo; repeat from * to last stitch, k1.

Row 16: K1, *k1, yo, k2, ssk, k3, k2tog, k2, yo; repeat from * to last stitch, k1.

Row 18: K1, *k1, yo, k3, ssk, k1, k2tog, k3, yo; repeat from * to last stitch, k1.

Row 20: K1, *k1, yo, k4, slip 1 as if to knit, k2tog, psso, k4, yo; repeat from * to last stitch, k1.

- □ k on RS, p on WS
- ⊡ yo
- ⧄ k2tog
- ⧅ ssk
- ⊠ sl 1 as if to knit, k2tog, psso

Leaning Squares (multiple of 16 + 1)

Rows 1, 3, 5, and 7 (RS): *(Ssk, yo) four times, k8; repeat from * to last stitch, k1.

Row 2 and all WS rows: Purl.

Rows 9, 11, 13, and 15: *K8, (yo, k2tog) four times; repeat from * to last stitch, k1.

Row 16: Purl.

Repeat Rows 1–16 for pattern.

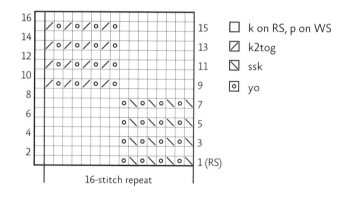

- □ k on RS, p on WS
- ⧄ k2tog
- ⧅ ssk
- ⊡ yo

16-stitch repeat

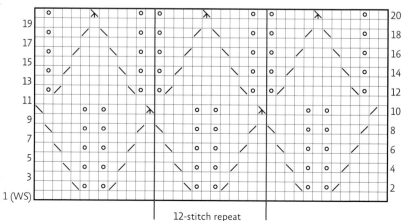

12-stitch repeat

GREEN TEA LACE WRISTLETS

The colorway used for these wristlets is very calm, so the irregular lace pattern is more easily visible. Wristlets are a great place to use the most luxurious yarns and colors—and a complex lace pattern.

SKILL LEVEL
Intermediate

SIZES
One Size

FINISHED MEASUREMENTS
7" circumference x 6" length

MATERIALS
- ArtYarns Regal Silk **3 LIGHT** (100% silk; 1¾ oz/50g, 163 yds/149m): 1 skein in Green, Green 119
- Set of four size 2 (2.75mm) double-pointed needles
- Waste yarn or stitch holder
- Tapestry needle

GAUGE
24 stitches and 32 rows = 4" in Ribbed-Lace Pattern

RIBBED LACE STITCH PATTERN (multiple of 4)

Round 1: *P2, yo, ssk; repeat from * around.

Round 2: *P2, k2; repeat from * around.

Round 3: *P2, k2tog, yo; repeat from * around.

Round 4: Repeat Round 2.

Repeat Rounds 1–4 for pattern.

	k on RS, p on WS
	p on RS, k on WS
╱	k2tog
╲	ssk
◯	yo

4-stitch repeat

NOTE

Pfb = Purl into front and back of stitch

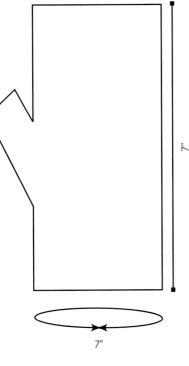

WRISTLET

Cast on 44 stitches. Divide onto three needles and join, being careful not to twist. Work in ribbed lace for 2".

THUMB GUSSET

Round 1: (Pfb) two times, work in pattern around—46 stitches.

Rounds 2–4: P4, work in pattern around.

Round 5: Pfb, p2, pfb, work in pattern around—48 stitches.

Rounds 6–8: P6, work in pattern around.

Round 9: Pfb, p4, pfb, work in pattern around—50 stitches.

Rounds 10–12: P8, work in pattern around.

Round 13: Pfb, p6, pfb, work in pattern around—52 stitches.

Rounds 14–16: P10, work in pattern around.

Round 17: Pfb, p8, pfb, work in pattern around—54 stitches.

Rounds 18–20: P12, work in pattern around.

Next round: P12, place these 12 stitches on holder, continue in pattern around. Cast on two stitches above thumb gusset and continue to work in pattern for 2½". Bind off.

THUMB

Place 12 stitches from holder onto two needles. Pick up and knit four stitches from two cast-on stitches above thumb—16 stitches. Work in reverse stockinette stitch for six rounds. Bind off.

Weave in ends. Block gently with steam, paying special attention to thumb so that it lies flat.

FIRESTORM LACE SHAWL

The shawl is knit in a repetitive lace pattern so any colorway will show off the lace stitch nicely. The colors in this variegated yarn are quite active and the fuzzy texture of the mohair yarn also tends to distract the eye from the lace design. Both are good reasons to use a repetitive lace pattern.

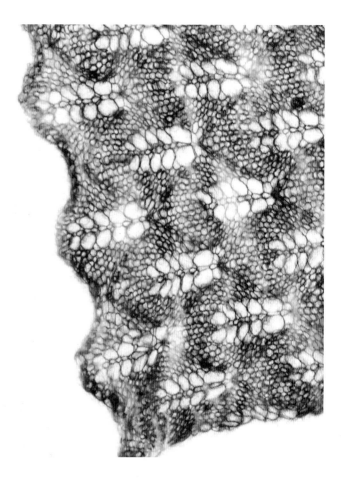

SKILL LEVEL
Intermediate

SIZES
One Size

FINISHED MEASUREMENTS
20" wide x 60" long after blocking

MATERIALS
- Lorna's Laces Heaven (90% kid mohair, 10% nylon; 7 oz/198g, 975 yds/891m): 1 skein Maple Grove
- One size 9 (5.5mm) 24" circular needle
- Tapestry needle

GAUGE
15 stitches and 24 rows = 4" in Diaphanous Lace Stitch Pattern, blocked

STITCH PATTERN
See Diaphanous Lace Stitch Pattern on page 124.

SHAWL
Cast on 74 stitches. Begin diaphanous lace pattern. Work even until piece measures 60" stretched to allow for blocking. Bind off all stitches. Weave in ends. Block thoroughly.

chapter

eleven

SAME COLORS, DIFFERENT YARNS

Mixing Weights and Textures

Many hand-dyed yarn companies offer the same colorway in several different yarn fibers and textures. Fibers such as silk and superwash wool absorb dye well, so the colors are intense, while the same colors in fuzzy mohair and angora are softened by the texture of the yarn. The variety of fibers and textures is great and by choosing two or more that are dyed in the same colorway, you know the yarns will complement each other. You can use the different yarns to make stripes by alternating as many textures as you like. Narrow stripes will appear to be one yarn from a distance but will prevent the colors from pooling.

Narrow Stripes

This swatch is knit in narrow two-row stripes in three different yarns—a smooth texture, a bouclé, and a mohair—all in the same colorway. The overall look is of a single yarn with lots of texture.

Garter-Stitch Stripes (any number of stitches)

A: Smooth texture

B: Bouclé texture

C: Mohair texture

Leave all yarns at the edge and carry them up the side.

Rows 1–2: With A, knit.

Rows 3–4: With B, knit.

Rows 5–6: With C, knit.

Repeat Rows 1–6 for pattern.

Wide Stripes

Wider stripes often show the different yarns more distinctly. And by working each yarn in a different stitch pattern, the textures are emphasized. The technique is subtle and can be used with any stitch pattern or design that you choose.

Striped Textures (odd number of stitches)

A: Smooth yarn

B: Fuzzy yarn

Rows 1 and 3 (RS): With A, knit.

Rows 2 and 4: With A, purl.

Rows 5–8: With B, *k1, p1; repeat from * to last stitch, k1.

Repeat Rows 1–8 for pattern.

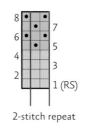

k on RS, p on WS

p on RS, k on RS

A

B

2-stitch repeat

Mixing Weights, Different Gauges

A creative way to mix yarns is to use different weight yarns in the same colorway, but because the yarns knit at different gauges, you need to compensate for that by working a very loose and open stitch with the lighter weight and using the heavier-weight yarn for the stabilizing portions.

Dropped-Stitch Pattern (any number of stitches)

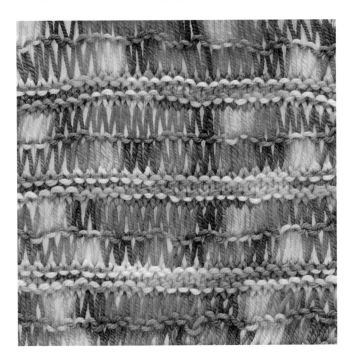

A: Worsted weight
B: DK weight
Rows 1–3: With A, knit.
Row 4: With B, knit in each stitch, wrapping yarn three times around needle.
Row 5: With B, knit in each stitch, wrapping yarn three times around needle, dropping extra wraps from previous row.
Row 6: With A, knit across, dropping extra wraps.
Repeat Rows 1–6 for pattern.

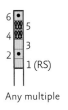

□ k on RS, p on WS
⊡ p on RS, k on RS
▨ knit, wrapping yarn 3 times around needle
▢ A
▢ B

Any multiple

Mixing Weights, Different Stitches

Another way to combine different weights of yarn is to use a stitch pattern that pulls in, such as ribbing, for the heavier-weight yarn and a stitch pattern that expands, such as garter stitch, for the lighter one. This way the two weights can be used at the same gauge.

Different-Weights Pattern (odd number of stitches)

A: Worsted weight
B: Bulky weight
Rows 1–4: With A, knit.
Rows 5, 7, and 9 (RS): With B, *k1, p1; repeat from * to last stitch, k1.
Rows 6, 8, and 10: With B, *p1, k1; repeat from * to last stitch, p1.
Repeat Rows 1–10 for pattern.

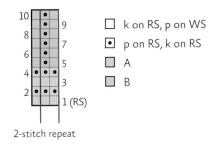

□ k on RS, p on WS
⊡ p on RS, k on RS
▢ A
▢ B

2-stitch repeat

Felting

A festive way to combine yarn textures is to use a felt-able wool for part of a project and the same color in a washable wool for another part. The washable wool could be used for the flap on a purse or the cuffs on slippers. The colors look a little different, but they work perfectly together.

Felted and Not Pattern

A: Feltable wool yarn
B: Superwash wool yarn
Using A, work in stockinette to desired size. Bind off. Felt in washing machine.
Using B, work other portions of project and attach after felting is complete.

Contrasting Trim

Knitting different sections of a project with a different texture yarn or a different weight yarn creates an entirely new look. The obvious places to do this are edgings, pockets, and collars, but you could also knit each sweater front in a different texture. Be as subtle or dramatic as you choose.

Trims and Edgings Pattern (any number of stitches)

A: Worsted weight
B: DK weight
With A, work main garment.
Use B for pockets, edgings, and trims.

POMEGRANATE TWEED TOTE

The three yarns used to knit this tote are all dyed in the same colorway. One of them is significantly thicker than the other two, so the lighter-weight ones are doubled to make the yarns more balanced. The thicker yarn also has less yardage, so it is used less frequently than the other two yarns.

SKILL LEVEL
Easy

FINISHED MEASUREMENTS
32" circumference x 15" tall

MATERIALS
- Mountain Colors Twizzle (4 MEDIUM) (A) (85% merino wool, 15% silk; 3 ½ oz/100g, 250 yds/229m): 2 skeins in Red Willow
- Mountain Colors Mountain Goat (4 MEDIUM) (B) (55% mohair, 45% wool; 3 ½ oz/100g, 230 yds/210m): 2 skeins in Red Willow
- Mountain Colors Moguls (5 BULKY) (C) (96% wool, 4% nylon; 3 ½ oz/100g, 65 yds/59m): 2 skeins in Red Willow
- Somerset Designs 12" x 4" leather tote bottom and one pair of 24" leather purse handles
- 1 yard cotton fabric for lining
- 1 yard 17" wide UltraBond Lite BondFusible Adhesive
- Size 10 (6mm) 29" circular needle
- Tapestry needle
- Sewing thread and needle
- Straight pins
- Iron

GAUGE

14 stitches and 28 rows = 4" in garter stitch

NOTES

Yarns A and B are used double throughout; yarn C is used single. Carry unused yarn loosely at the edge of the work.

YARN REPEAT

Rows 1–4: With A, knit.
Rows 5–8: With B, knit.
Rows 9–10: With C, knit.
Repeat Rows 1–10 for yarn repeat.

With A and circular needle, cast on 112 stitches. Do not join. Knit back and forth in garter stitch following Yarn Repeat until piece measures 15" from cast-on. Bind off all stitches. There is no need to weave in ends, as they can be fused between the knitting and the lining.

LINING

Block the rectangle to measure exactly 32" wide. Iron the fabric lining and cut to the exact height of the knit rectangle and 34" wide. If pockets are desired, cut the pockets, turn the edges under and sew to the right side of the lining. Cut fusible adhesive to the same size as the lining and fuse to the wrong side of the fabric, following the instructions on the package. Peel off the paper backing. Position the knit rectangle wrong side up on a flat surface. Place the lining on the knit rectangle, fusible side down. Line up all the edges with 2" of width over-hanging one edge. Fuse thoroughly from the fabric side, being very careful not to fuse the 2" overlap. Roll up the project into a tube, butting the knit edges together. With right sides facing and yarn A, sew the knit edges together. Place the iron inside this tube to fuse the 2" overlap across the seam. Do not turn the bag inside out to fuse.

Place the lined knitting into the leather tote bottom. Pin it in place, then sew it on by hand. Pin the handles in place and check the height. Sew the handles in place.

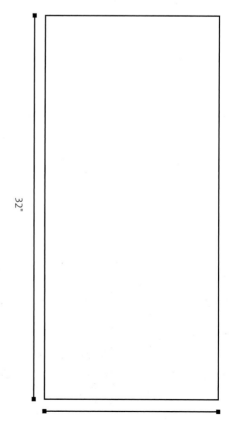

32"

15 "

DAYBREAK TEXTURED THROW

One yarn company not only dyes a dozen different yarn textures in the same color-way, it packages them together, ready to use. This throw begins in the center, growing outward. Each of the twelve yarns is used until it runs out, which does not have to be at the beginning of a round. Fewer textures could also be used, again changing yarns as desired or simply when one yarn runs out.

SKILL LEVEL
Easy

SIZES
One Size

FINISHED MEASUREMENTS
48" square, blocked

MATERIALS
- Hand Painted Knitting Yarns Giant Skein (20 oz/567g, 1440 yds/1317m) in Parsifal Pastel. Each skein contains 120 yards each of the following 12 yarns:
  - Cestari (100% merino wool)
  - Bouclé (54% mohair, 23% silk, 18% wool, 5% nylon)
  - Glitter (95% merino wool, 5% Lurex)
  - Celebration (78% mohair, 13% wool, 9% nylon)
  - Stream (55% mohair, 45% merino wool)
  - Kid Mohair/Silk (71% kid mohair, 21% silk, 8% nylon)
  - Merino/Bamboo (60% merino wool, 40% bamboo)
  - Fantasia (45% merino wool, 55% nylon)
  - Tweed (100% lambs wool)
  - Precious (50% silk, 50% merino wool)
  - Glitter Bouclé (45% mohair, 45% merino wool, 10% nylon)
  - Hand Spun Merino (100% merino wool)
- Set of 5 size 8 (5mm) double-pointed needles
- Size 10 (6mm) 16" circular needle
- Size 10 (6mm) 32" circular needle
- Stitch markers in 2 colors
- Tapestry needle

GAUGE
Gauge varies with yarn, but approximately 16 stitches and 20 rounds = 4" in stockinette stitch

SEED STITCH PATTERN
(even number of stitches)
Round 1: *K1, p1; repeat from * around.
Round 2: *P1, k1; repeat from * around.
Repeat Rounds 1–2 for pattern.

NOTES
The throw begins in the center and increases at each of the four corners every other round. Choose the yarns in any order. With each yarn change, also change the stitch, alternating stockinette stitch with seed stitch. Be careful not to drop the yarn-over at the end of the double-pointed needles.

THROW

With any yarn and double-pointed needles, cast on eight stitches. Divide evenly onto four needles and join for working in the round, being careful not to twist. Place marker to indicate beginning of round. Knit one round.

Round 1: *K1, yo; repeat from * around.
Round 2: Knit.
Round 3: *K1, yo, k3, yo; repeat from * 3 times.
Round 4: Knit.
Round 5: *K1, yo, k5, yo; repeat from * 3 times.
Round 6: Knit.

Place removable markers through each of the knit-one corner stitches, using a different-colored one for the beginning of the round. Continue to work one plain round alternating with an increase round until 5" of this yarn remains and changing to circular needles as the piece gets larger. Join next yarn and begin seed stitch. Continue in seed stitch while working yarn over increases at each corner as established until 5" of this yarn remains. Continue to join new yarns and alternate between stockinette stitch and seed stitch for each yarn. For last yarn, work until approximately 20 yards remain. Bind off loosely. Weave in ends. Block to shape.

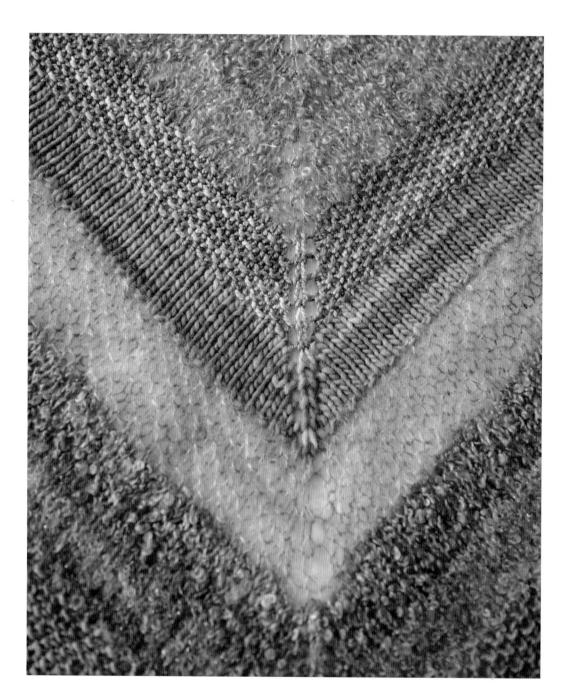

Skill Levels

Easy. Uses basic stitches, repetitive stitch patterns, and simple color changes. Involves simple shaping and finishing.

Intermediate. Uses a variety of stitches, such as basic cables and lace, simple intarsia, double-pointed needles, and knitting-in-the-round needle techniques, with midlevel shaping and finishing.

Experienced. Involves intricate stitch patterns, techniques, and dimension, such as non-repeating patterns, multi-colored techniques, fine threads, detailed shaping, and refined finishing.

Yarn Substitutions

The patterns in this book were each designed with a specific yarn in mind. If you substitute for a recommended yarn, you should choose one with the same weight and a similar fiber content. You should always take the time to make a gauge swatch before you begin a pattern, but it's especially important to do so if you are substituting for the suggested yarn. If necessary, change needle sizes to obtain the correct gauge.

Yarn Weight Categories

	Types of yarn in category	Knit gauge range (in Stockinette stitch to 4 inches)	Recommended needle sizes (U.S./metric sizes)
0 LACE	Fingering, 10-count crochet thread	33–40 sts	000–1/1.5–2.25mm
1 SUPER FINE	Sock, fingering, baby	27–32 sts	1–3/2.25–3.25mm
2 FINE	Sport, baby	23–26 sts	3–5/3.25–3.75mm
3 LIGHT	DK, light worsted	21–24 sts	5–7/3.75–4.5mm
4 MEDIUM	Worsted, afghan, aran	16–20 sts	7–9/4.5–5.5mm
5 BULKY	Chunky, craft, rug	12–15 sts	9–11/5.5–8mm
6 SUPER BULKY	Bulky, roving	6–11 sts	11 and larger/8mm and larger

Adapted from the Standard Yarn Weight System of the Craft Yarn Council of America (www.yarnstandards.com)

Knitting Abbreviations

Note: Special abbreviations are defined in the patterns.

* * = repeat steps between asterisks as many times as indicated
CC = contrast color
dec = decrease
est = established
g = gram(s)
inc = increase
k = knit
k2tog = knit 2 together
kfb = knit into front and back of next stitch
m = meter(s)
MC = main color
mm = millimeter
oz = ounce(s)
p = purl
p2tog = purl 2 together
pfb = purl into front and back of stitch
pm = place marker
psso = pass slipped stitch over
rep = repeat
rnd = round
RS = right side
ssk = slip, slip, knit
st(s) = stitch(es)
tbl = through the back loop
WS = wrong side
wyib = with yarn in back
wyif = with yarn in front
yd(s) = yard(s)
yo = yarn over

Metric Conversion Chart

Inches to Centimeters

inches	cm	inches	cm
$\frac{1}{16}$	0.16	27	60.58
$\frac{1}{8}$	0.32	28	71.12
$\frac{3}{16}$	0.48	29	73.66
$\frac{1}{4}$	0.64	30	76.20
$\frac{5}{16}$	0.79	31	78.74
$\frac{3}{8}$	0.95	32	81.28
$\frac{7}{16}$	1.11	33	83.82
$\frac{1}{2}$	1.27	34	86.36
$\frac{9}{16}$	1.43	35	88.9
$\frac{5}{8}$	1.59	36	91.44
$\frac{11}{16}$	1.75	37	93.98
$\frac{3}{4}$	1.91	38	96.52
$\frac{13}{16}$	2.06	39	99.06
$\frac{7}{8}$	2.22	40	101.60
$\frac{15}{16}$	2.38	41	104.14
1	2.54	42	106.68
2	5.08	43	109.22
3	7.65	44	111.76
4	10.16	45	114.30
5	12.70	46	116.84
6	15.24	47	119.38
7	17.78	48	121.92
8	20.32	49	124.46
9	22.66	50	127.00
10	25.40	51	129.54
11	27.94	52	132.08
12	30.48	53	134.62
13	33.02	54	137.16
14	35.56	55	139.70
15	38.10	56	142.24
16	40.64	57	144.78
17	43.18	58	147.32
18	45.72	59	149.86
19	48.26	60	152.40
20	50.80		
21	53.34		
22	55.88		
23	58.42		
24	60.96		
25	63.50		
26	66.04		

Centimeters to Inches

cm	inches	cm	inches	cm	inches	cm	inches
1	$\frac{3}{8}$	42	16 $\frac{1}{2}$	83	32 $\frac{5}{8}$	124	48 $\frac{7}{8}$
2	$\frac{3}{4}$	43	16 $\frac{7}{8}$	84	33	125	49 $\frac{1}{4}$
3	1 $\frac{1}{8}$	44	17 $\frac{1}{4}$	85	33 $\frac{1}{2}$	126	49 $\frac{5}{8}$
4	1 $\frac{5}{8}$	45	17 $\frac{3}{4}$	86	33 $\frac{7}{8}$	127	50
5	2	46	18 $\frac{1}{8}$	87	34 $\frac{1}{4}$	128	50 $\frac{3}{8}$
6	2 $\frac{3}{8}$	47	18 $\frac{1}{2}$	88	34 $\frac{5}{8}$	129	50 $\frac{3}{4}$
7	2 $\frac{1}{4}$	48	18 $\frac{7}{8}$	89	35	130	51 $\frac{1}{8}$
8	3 $\frac{1}{8}$	49	19 $\frac{1}{4}$	90	35 $\frac{1}{2}$	131	51 $\frac{5}{8}$
9	3 $\frac{1}{2}$	50	19 $\frac{5}{8}$	91	35 $\frac{7}{8}$	132	52
10	4	51	20	92	36 $\frac{1}{4}$	133	52 $\frac{3}{8}$
11	4 $\frac{3}{8}$	52	20 $\frac{1}{2}$	93	36 $\frac{5}{8}$	134	52 $\frac{3}{4}$
12	4 $\frac{3}{4}$	53	20 $\frac{7}{8}$	94	37	135	53 $\frac{1}{8}$
13	5 $\frac{1}{8}$	54	21 $\frac{1}{4}$	95	37 $\frac{3}{8}$	136	53 $\frac{1}{2}$
14	5 $\frac{1}{2}$	55	21 $\frac{5}{8}$	96	37 $\frac{3}{4}$	137	58 $\frac{7}{8}$
15	5 $\frac{7}{8}$	56	22	97	38 $\frac{1}{4}$	138	54 $\frac{3}{8}$
16	6 $\frac{1}{4}$	57	22 $\frac{1}{2}$	98	38 $\frac{5}{8}$	139	54 $\frac{3}{4}$
17	6 $\frac{3}{4}$	58	22 $\frac{7}{8}$	99	39	140	55 $\frac{1}{8}$
18	7 $\frac{1}{8}$	59	23 $\frac{1}{4}$	100	39 $\frac{3}{8}$	141	55 $\frac{1}{2}$
19	7 $\frac{1}{2}$	60	23 $\frac{5}{8}$	101	39 $\frac{3}{4}$	142	55 $\frac{7}{8}$
20	7 $\frac{7}{8}$	61	24	102	40 $\frac{1}{8}$	143	56 $\frac{1}{2}$
21	8 $\frac{1}{4}$	62	24 $\frac{3}{8}$	103	40 $\frac{1}{2}$	144	56 $\frac{3}{4}$
22	8 $\frac{5}{8}$	63	24 $\frac{3}{4}$	104	41	145	57
23	9	64	25 $\frac{1}{4}$	105	41 $\frac{3}{8}$	146	57 $\frac{1}{2}$
24	9 $\frac{1}{2}$	65	25 $\frac{5}{8}$	106	41 $\frac{3}{4}$	147	57 $\frac{7}{8}$
25	9 $\frac{7}{8}$	66	26	107	42 $\frac{1}{8}$	148	58 $\frac{1}{4}$
26	10 $\frac{1}{4}$	67	26 $\frac{3}{8}$	108	42 $\frac{1}{2}$	149	58 $\frac{5}{8}$
27	10 $\frac{5}{8}$	68	26 $\frac{3}{4}$	109	42 $\frac{7}{8}$	150	59
28	11	69	27 $\frac{1}{8}$	110	43 $\frac{1}{4}$	151	59 $\frac{1}{2}$
29	11 $\frac{3}{8}$	70	27 $\frac{1}{2}$	111	43 $\frac{3}{4}$	152	59 $\frac{7}{8}$
30	11 $\frac{7}{8}$	71	28	112	44 $\frac{1}{8}$	153	60 $\frac{1}{4}$
31	12 $\frac{1}{4}$	72	28 $\frac{3}{8}$	113	44 $\frac{1}{2}$		
32	12 $\frac{5}{8}$	73	28 $\frac{3}{4}$	114	44 $\frac{7}{8}$		
33	13	74	29 $\frac{1}{8}$	115	45 $\frac{1}{4}$		
34	13 $\frac{3}{8}$	75	29 $\frac{1}{2}$	116	45 $\frac{5}{8}$		
35	13 $\frac{3}{4}$	76	29 $\frac{7}{8}$	117	46		
36	14 $\frac{1}{8}$	77	30 $\frac{1}{4}$	118	46 $\frac{1}{2}$		
37	14 $\frac{5}{8}$	78	30 $\frac{3}{4}$	119	46 $\frac{7}{8}$		
38	15	79	31 $\frac{1}{8}$	120	47 $\frac{1}{4}$		
39	15 $\frac{3}{8}$	80	31 $\frac{1}{2}$	121	47 $\frac{5}{8}$		
40	15 $\frac{3}{4}$	81	31 $\frac{7}{8}$	122	48		
41	16 $\frac{1}{8}$	82	32 $\frac{1}{4}$	123	48 $\frac{3}{8}$		

Knitting Needle Conversion Chart

Metric Sizes	U.S. Sizes	UK/Canadian Sizes
2 mm	0	14
2.25 mm	1	13
2.75 mm	2	12
3.25 mm	3	10
3.5 mm	4	-
3.75 mm	5	9
4 mm	6	8
4.5 mm	7	7
5 mm	8	6
5.5 mm	9	5
6 mm	10	4
6.5 mm	10½	3
8 mm	11	0
9 mm	13	00
10 mm	15	000
12.75 mm	17	0000
15 mm	19	00000
19 mm	35	-
25 mm	50	-

Resources

ArtYarns
39 Westmoreland Avenue
White Plains, NY 10606
914-428-0333
www.artyarns.com

Brown Sheep
100662 County Road 16
Mitchell, NE 69357
800-826-91636
www.brownsheep.com

Farmhouse Yarns
283 Mount Parnassus Road
East Haddam, CT 06423
860-575-9050
www.farmhouseyarns.com

Fiesta Yarns
5401 San Diego Avenue NE
Albuquerque, NM 87113
505-892-5008
www.fiestayarns.com

Hand Painted Knitting Yarns
1006 Morgan Meadow Drive
Wentzville, MO 63385
636-332-9931
www.handpaintedknitting-
yarns.com

Jade Sapphire Exotic Fibres
West Nyack, NY 10994
845-215-9946
www.jadesapphire.com

JHB International, Inc.
1955 South Quince Street
Denver, CO 80231
800-525-9007
www.buttons.com

Lorna's Laces
4229 North Honore Street
Chicago, IL 60613
773-935-3803
www.lornaslaces.net

Mountain Colors
P.O. Box 156
Corvallis, MT 59828
406-961-1900
www.mountaincolors.com

Prism Yarn
3140 39th Avenue North
St. Petersburg, FL 33714
727-528-3800
www.prismyarn.com

Schaefer Yarn Company
3514 Kelly's Corners Road
Interlaken, NY 14847
607-532-9452
www.schaeferyarn.com

Somerset Designs
P.O. Box 425
Somerset, CA 95684
530-622-6898
www.somersetdesigns.com

Sunbelt Fastener Company
8841 Exposition Boulevard
Culver City, CA 90230
310-836-5212
www.sunbeltfastener.com

Twisted Sisters
740 Metcalf Street #21
Escondido, CA 92025
760-489-8846
www.TwistedSistersKnitting.
com

Zipperstop
27 Allen Street
New York, NY 10002
212-226-3964
www.zipperstop.com

Index